Per T. Cleve

On some new and little known diatoms.

Communicated to the Royal Swedish Academy of Sciences September 15,

1880

Per T. Cleve

On some new and little known diatoms.
Communicated to the Royal Swedish Academy of Sciences September 15, 1880

ISBN/EAN: 9783337724467

Printed in Europe, USA, Canada, Australia, Japan

Cover: Foto ©ninafisch / pixelio.de

More available books at **www.hansebooks.com**

ON SOME NEW AND LITTLE KNOWN DIATOMS

BY

P. T. CLEVE.

WITH SIX PLATES.

COMMUNICATED TO THE ROYAL SWEDISH ACADEMY OF SCIENCES SEPTEMBER 15, 1880.

STOCKHOLM, 1881.
KONGL. BOKTRYCKERIET.
P. A. NORSTEDT & SÖNER.

Several years ago I received through Professor S. Lovén from the Swedish State Museum some samples af shellsand and mud, which had been collected during the expedition of the Roy. Swedish Fregatè *Eugenie* 1851—53 on the Gallapagos Islands, Honolulu, Port Jackson etc. On examining these samples, as well as many others, received from various friends and correspondents, I found a number of diatoms, which seems to me to be entirely new to science or at least of interest. Especially am I indebted to Dr. Söderlund for some very rich materials from the Mediterranean Sea and the Balearic Islets, to Mr. Christian Febiger, the wellknown diatomist of Wilmington, Delaware, Mr. Hauck of Triest, Prof. Berggren, Dr. O. Nordstedt and others for various interesting gatherings. Mr. Grunow of Vienna has kindly helped me in preparing this paper and assisted me in many cases of uncertainity, and for which I here take the liberty of tendering him my best thanks.

Mastogloia Thwaites.

1. *M. panduriformis* Cl. N. Sp.

Valve panduriform with cuneate ends. Margin with somewhat distant loculi, except in the middle, on both sides of the central nodule, where they are wanting or indiscernible. The surface of the valve is covered with small, irregularly scattered puncta and very fine (20 in 0,01 mm.), parallel, punctate striæ. These striæ, which are not strongly marked, cover the whole valve, except a small area, round the straight median line and central nodule. Terminal nodules turned in opposite directions.

Length 0,0975 mm. Breadth 0,027 mm. at the constriction 0,0195 mm.

Gallapagos Islands (Eugenie Exp.) Very rare.

Pl. I, fig. 1, $^{800}/_1$.

The outline of the frustule, the few and large loculi as well as its peculiar structure destinguishes this fine form from all previously known species. Its nearest allies are the Naviculæ or Mastogloiæ, forming A. Schmidts section Pseudodiploneis, *N. marginata* Lewis, *N. strangulata* Grev., *Mastogl.? reticulata* Grun.

2. *Mastogloia submarginata* CL. et GRUN. N. Sp.

Elliptic lanceolate, ends neither produced nor capitate. Marginal loculi very indistinct, 5—8 in 0,01 mm. Striæ punctate, 18—20 in 0,01 mm., most strongly marked near the margin and on both sides of the median line, so that they seem to be interrupted by a more or less large lunate area. The striæ continue across this area, but are very faintly marked, and can only be discovered with good objectives.

Length 0,04—0,048 mm. Breadth 0,013—0,017 mm.

Gallapagos Islands (Eugenie Exp.), Campêche Bay (accord. to GRUNOW).

Pl. I, fig. 2, $^{1000}/_1$.

The specimens from Gallapagos Islands have 18 striæ and 8 canaliculi in 0,01 mm., specimens from Campêche Bay, according to GRUNOW, 20 striæ and 5—7 canaliculi. In its very indistinct canaliculi and the interrupted striæ this species comes nearest to *N. Jelineckii* GRUN.

Amphora EHB.

1. *A. Berggrenii* CL. N. Sp.

Median band not complex, central nodule not transversely dilated. The frustule is elongated with broad and rounded ends and almost parallel sides; its form being like that of *A. arenaria* DONK. The valve is striate, dorsal striæ almost parallel, more distant in the middle (17 in 0,01 mm.) than near the ends (20 in 0,01 mm.); ventral striæ irregular, divergent, especially near the terminal nodules. Terminal nodules conspicuous and seem to project into the frustule.

Length of the frustule 0,065 mm. Breadth 0,025 mm.

Fossil, Arthurs Pass, New Zeeland, mixed with freshwater species, such as *Navicula serians*, *N. rhomboides*, *N. cuspidata* etc. S. BERGGREN.

Pl. I, fig. 3, $^{1000}/_1$; *a.* valve, *b.* frustule.

A freshwater species of Amphora having this appearance is very remarkable. I have issued this species in CL. et MÖLL. Diat. N:o 90.

Cymbella AG.

1. *Cymbella Brasiliana* CL. N. Sp.

Almost symmetrical, naviculoid (a faint obliquity being percebtible only on large specimens), lanceolate with somewhat obtuse apices. Median line straight. Striæ radiant, near the apices almost parallel, covering the whole surface, except a narrow (larger near the central nodule), area round the median line. The central striæ are stronger and more marked than the others. All the striæ are punctate, the puncta forming wawy longitudinal lines. Striæ 22 in 0,01 mm. on the part between the middle and the ends.

Length 0,035 -0,06 mm. Breadth 0,012—0,015 mm.
Pl. I, fig. 4, a. (dry), b. (balsam); $^{1000}/_1$.
Brazil, fresh water, collected by Dr. WARMING. (CL. et MÖLL. Diat. N:o 193.)
In the strongly marked central striæ this form reminds one of *Navicula Crucicula*, but it is quite different. There is also some resemblance to the *Navicula Lundströmii* CL. (in CL. et GRUN. Arctische Diat. Pl. III, fig. 39). Another allied form is the as yet undescribed *Cymbella Frieseana* GRUN. from Tana Elf in Finmarken (CL. et MÖLL. Diat. N:o 261). This species has produced and capitate ends and 12—15 punctate striæ in the middle, 18—19 halfway between the middle and the ends, where they are 21 in 0,01 mm. Length 0,05—0,06 mm. Breadth 0,014 mm.

2. *Cymbella Stodderi* CL. N. Sp.
Elongate, lanceolate, slightly asymmetrical. Ends slightly produced and attenuated. Striæ strongly radiant in the middle, almost parallel near the apices, scarcely punctate, 10 in 0,01 mm. a little more distant in the centre, covering $^2/_3$ of the valve and leaving on both sides of the median line a tolerably broad area.
Length 0,075—0,09 mm. Breadth 0,015 mm.
Pl. I, fig. 5; $^{1000}/_1$ (Specimen from Brazil).
Fossil: Bemis Lake in White Mountains (Mr. STODDER). Living: Brazil, Minas Geraes on Sphagna leg. Dr. HJ. MOSÉN.
This species, which occurs in CL. et MÖLL. Diat. N:o 212 and N:o 274, is most nearly related to the *C. Americana* A. SCHM. Atl. Pl. IX, fig. 15 and 20, but the latter form has a more narrow area and, as fig. 15 shows, punctate striæ.

Pleurosigma W. SM.

1. *Pleurosigma tortuosum* CL. N. Sp.
Median line strongly and equally sigmoid. Striæ in three sets, oblique 21, transverse 22 in 0,01 mm.
Length 0,076 mm. Breadth 0,008 mm.
Pl. I, fig. 6; $^{1000}/_1$.
Balearic Islets (Dr. SÖDERLUND) rare.

2. *Pleurosigma lanceolatum* var. *cuspidatum* CL.
Lanceolate with produced apices, symmetrical. Median line straight, the ends turned in opposite directions. Striæ in three sets, one transverse (20 in 0,01 mm.) and two oblique (22 in 0,01 mm.).
Length 0,083 mm. Breadth 0,02 mm.
Pl. I, fig. 7; $^{1000}/_1$. b. structure; $^{2000}/_1$.
Marine: Port Jackson (Eugenie Exp.).
The same variety from Newcastle has according to GRUNOW 20 transverse and 19 oblique striæ in 0,01 mm. Length 0,105 mm. Breadth 0,026 mm.

3. *Pleurosigma (Donkinia?) longissimum* CL. N. Sp.

Very long and narrow, linear; ends obtuse. Median line straight in the middle but curved in the last third part from the central nodule. Striæ in two sets crossing each other in right angles, transverse $18^1/_2$, longitudinal 21 in 0,01 mm. Colour pale straw.

Length of the frustule 0,17 mm. Breadth 0,0083 mm.

Pl. I, fig. 8. *a.* $^{500}/_1$; *b.* structure $^{2000}/_1$.

Balearic Islets rare (leg. Dr. SÖDERLUND).

Rhoicosigma GRUN.

1. *Rhoicosigma mediterraneum* CL. (in GRUN. Micr. Journ. 1877, p. 182).

Narrow lanceolate, with acute ends. Median line strongly bent in the first third part from the central nodule, afterwords straight. Striæ longitudinal and transverse. The longitudinal striæ are very fine, about 27 in 0,01 mm., the transverse $18^1/_2$ in 0,01 mm.

Length 0,18—0,21 mm. Breadth 0,0225 mm.

Pl. I, fig. 9, $^{511}/_1$. *a.* and *b.* valves, *c.* structure $^{3000}/_1$.

Balearic Islets rare (leg. Dr. SÖDERLUND).

Navicula BORY.

1. *Navicula (Fluminensis* var.?) *Floridana* CL. N. Sp.

Elongated, slightly constricted in the middle, ends rounded. Striæ not distinctly punctate, parallel, 15 in 0,01 mm., closer near the ends, 20 in 0,01 mm., absent from the middle part of the valve, not reaching the median line, which is surrounded by a narrow, linear area.

Length 0,045—0,075 mm. Breadth 0,01—0,012 mm. at the constriction 0,08—0,009 mm.

Pl. I, fig. 10, $^{1000}/_1$.

Florida coast, near Pensacola Harbour (in a gathering sent by Mr. FEBIGER).

2. *Navicula cruciata* CL. N. Sp.

Oblong, slightly contracted at the centre. Striæ 12 in 0,01 mm., parallel, costate, smooth or indistinctly granulate, absent from the middle part of the valve, not reaching the median line.

Length 0,087 mm. Breadth 0,017 mm. at the middle 0,014 mm.

Pl. I, Fig. 11, $^{1000}/_1$.

I have found this species in a sample, said to be from Greenland, but as it contained many tropical forms, I am not sure that this is correct.

3. *Navicula Grœnlandica* CL. N. Sp.

Lanceolate with obtuse apices. Striæ coarse, costate, very radiant and divergent, crowded around the centre of the valve ($7^1/_2$ in 0,01 mm.) more distant between the centre and the ends (6 in 0,01 mm.), interrupted by furrows, parallel to the margins. Around the central nodule there is a very large orbicular area.
Length 0,117 mm. Breadth 0,023 mm.
Pl. I, fig. 13, $^{1000}/_1$.
Greenland, Davis Strait (very rare in CL. et MÖLL. Diat. N:o 172).

In its characters this species approches *N. Trevelyana*, but its form is entirely different. The striæ are also more distant, being in *N. Trevelyana* 10 in 0,01 mm. The terminal nodules of *N. Grœnlandia* are peculiar and resemble those of *N. Regula* CL. et GRUN. (CL. W. Ind. Diat. p. 5, Pl. 1, fig. 3.)

4. *Navicula Eugeniæ* CL. N. Sp.

Valve very convex, linear, with rounded ends. Striæ coarse, costate, radiant, 9 in 0,01 mm., reaching the median line, interrupted by a line parallel to the margin. Median line undulate. Central nodule surrounded by a small area. Terminal nodules elongated. — F. V. Frustule constricted in the middle; ends truncate.
Length 0,085—0,1 mm. Breadth 0,017 mm.
Pl. II, fig. 16, $^{1000}/_1$, *a*. S. V., *b*. F. V.
Gallapagos Islands (Eugenie Exp.).

5. *Navicula Hennedyi* var. *undulata* CL.

Oval with cunate ends and three undulations on each side. Striæ distinctly punctate, marginal and around the median line. The striæ near the median line are 16 in 0,01 mm. as are also the marginal striæ, except in the constrictions between the undulations, where they are only 12 in 0,01 mm.
Length 0,07 mm. Breadth 0,035 mm.
Pl. II, fig. 19, $^{1000}/_1$.
Gallapagos Islands (Eugenie Exp.).

This variety has finer striæ than the other forms of the most variable N. Hennedyi; the outline is also different.

N. Hennedyi var. *minuta* CL.

Broadly oval, with the marginal punctate striæ (7—8 in 0,01 mm.) separated from each other by unusually large spaces. Central striæ 9—10 in 0,01 mm.
Length 0,05 mm. Breadth 0,027 mm.
Pl. I, fig. 15, $^{1000}/_1$.
Gallapagos Islands (Eugenie Exp.).

N. Hennedyi var. *Tahitensis* Cl.

Broadly oval with almost parallel sides. Striæ scarcely punctate, marginal 13 in 0,01 mm., central 15 in 0,01 mm.
Length 0,05 mm. Breadth 0,023 mm.
Pl. I, fig. 14, $^{1000}/_1$.
Tahiti (Eugenie Exp.).
This variety is remarkable for its almost smooth striæ.

6. *Navicula rudis* Cl. N. Sp.

Broadly oval, with broadly rounded ends. Striæ coarse, 6 in 0,01 mm. marginal composed of about 5—8 large, separate puncta; central striæ composed of 2—3 puncta.
Length 0,052 mm. Breadth 0,032 mm.
Pl. II, fig. 17, $^{1000}/_1$.
Balearic Islets rare (leg. Dr. Söderlund).

This peculiar form belongs evidently to the *Nav. Lyra* section. It approaches in some respects *N. spectabilis* Greg. and *N. prætexta* Ehb., but it differs of both.

The numerous forms, belonging to this section, are so closely allied, that it is impossible to decide what are species or what varieties. Another most beautiful and gigantic form of this section is the following:

7. *Navicula* (*excavata* Grev. var.?) *Angelorum* Cl.

Very large, broadly oval, with rounded ends. Area large bilobate. Striæ punctate, radiant, $6^1/_2$ in 0,01 mm. (8 near the ends). Central striæ $11^1/_2$ in 0,01 mm.
Length 0,22 mm. Breadth 0,12 mm.
Pl. II, fig. 20, $^{600}/_1$.
Fossil: California, Sancta Monica los Angelos (comm. by Dr. G. Eisen).

8. *Navicula Holmiensis* Cl.

Valve large, oblong elliptic, with rounded ends. Striæ slightly radiant, $12^1/_2$ in 0,01 mm., indistinctly punctate, covering a little more than half the valve and leaving round the median line an irregular area.
Length 0,07—01 mm. Breadth in 0,023 mm.
Pl. II, fig. 18, $^{1000}/_1$.
Slightly brackish water near Waxholm (entrence to Stockholm) leg. Lagerstedt and O. Nordstedt.

This form agrees in general appearance with *N. latiuscula* Kütz. (*N. patula* W. Sm.), but has more distant striæ, which in *N. latiuscula* are 18 in 0,01 mm. and parallel.

9. *Navicula Platessa* Cl. N. Sp.

Small, broadly elliptic, with mucronate apices. Striæ strong, smooth, 8 in 0,01 mm., marginal, leaving around the median line a very large area.
Length 0,028 mm. Breadth 0,018 mm.
Pl. I, fig. 12, $^{1000}/_1$.
Gallapagos Islands rare (Eugenie Exp.).

This little Navicula belong to the Palpebralis-group, but differs from all described forms of that section by its short, distant and coarse striæ.

10. *Navicula Hauckii* Cl. N. Sp.

Very long and slender, linear, somewhat gibbous in the middle and near the ends, convex. Striæ punctate, 15 in the middle of the valve, 16 towards the ends and 18 in 0,01 mm. in the ends, a little shortened around the central nodule and not reaching the median line, which is surrounded by a linear area. The striæ are interrupted by a very fine line parallel with the margin.
Length 0,128 mm. Breadth 0,012 mm.
Pl. II, fig. 27, $^{900}/_1$.
Adriatic Sea, Rovigno, stomachs of Holothurians. leg. F. Hauck (rare in Cl. et Möll. Diat. N:o 208—210).

This species seems to belong to the section *Nav. limosæ* and is allied to *N. maxima*, *N. formosa* etc.

11. *Navicula Febigerii* Cl. N. Sp.

Lanceolate, with produced, obtuse ends. Striæ 16 in 0,01 mm., composed of distinct puncta, reaching the median line. In the middle they are alternately longer and shorter around the central nodule, which is surrounded by a broad area.
Length 0,054 mm. Breadth 0,02 mm.
Pl. II, fig. 21, $^{1000}/_1$.
Oakland Bridge, California in a sample sent by Mr. Chr. Febiger.

This beautiful little species has some resemblance to *Achnanthes Danica* (Flögel) Grun., but seems to be a true Navicula, belonging to the section »punctatæ«.

12. *Navicula Cluthensis* var.? *maculifera* Cl.

Broadly oval, with rounded ends. Striæ radiant, reaching the median line, abbreviated around the central nodule, which is surrounded by a tolerably large area. Number of striæ, (which are composed of distinct puncta), 11—12 in 0,01 mm.
Length 0,05 mm. Breadth 0,026 mm.
Pl. II, fig. 23, $^{1900}/_1$.
Slightly brackish water, near Waxholm, entrance to Stockholm (Mr. Lagerstedt).

This form has closer striæ than the typical species and an area around the nodule. Another smaller form is probably.

N. *Cluthensis* var. *minuta* CL.

Broadly oval, with rounded ends. Striæ slightly radiant, composed of distinct puncta, abbreviate around the central nodule, 15 in 0,01 mm. in the middle, 18 in 0,01 mm. in the ends.
Length 0,03 mm. Breadth 0,014 mm.
Pl. II, fig. 22, $^{1000}/_1$.
Florida, Pensacola in a gathering, sent by Mr. CHR. FEBIGER.
The following varieties of N. *Cluthensis* are described:
 a. *genuina* (GREG. Diat. of Clyde p. 6, Pl. I, fig. 2) with 8 striæ in 0,01 mm and no area. Length 0,035—0,04 mm.
 b. *erythræa* (N. *erythræa* GRUN. Verh. 1860 p. 539, Pl. III, fig. 17) with 10—12 striæ in 0,01 mm. and no area. Length 0,05—0,06 mm.
 c. *Finmarchica* GRUN. (in CL. et GRUN. Arct. Diat. p. 40, Pl. II, fig. 49) with 11—12 striæ in 0,01 mm. and very small area. Length 0,022—0,024 mm.
 d. *maculifera* CL. with 11 striæ in 0,01 mm. and tolerably large area.
 e. *minuta* CL. with 15—18 striæ in 0,01 mm. and tolerably large area.

13. *Navicula bicuspidata* CL. et GRUN.

Oblong, slightly constricted in the middle, apiculate. Striæ coarse, finely punctate, 6 in 0,01 mm., shortened around the middle.
Length 0,04 mm. Breadth 0,015 mm.
Pl. II, fig. 25, $^{1000}/_1$.
Mediterranean, Pithuisian Islands in a gathering sent by Prof. V. B. WITTROCK.
The nearest allied to this species seems to be *Nav. directa* SM. The *Nav. salva* A. SCHM. and *Nav. opima* GRUN. have the terminal nodules at some distance from the apices.

14. *Navicula mesoleia* CL. N. Sp.

Very convex, linear with cuneate ends. Striæ coarse, 15 in 0,01 mm., very slightly radiant, almost reaching the median line, absent from the middle of the valve, where there is a transverse blank space.
Length 0,04—0,06 mm. Breadth 0,005—0,008 mm.
Pl. II, fig. 26 a and b, $^{1000}/_1$.
Fresh water, Brazil, leg Dr. WARMING. (CL. et MÖLL. Diat. N:o 193.)
This form has the appearance of some smaller varieties of N. *Pinnularia* CL. (CL. et GRUN. Arct. Diat. p. 27) but is more convex and has closer striæ.

15. *Navicula Fromenteræ* CL. N. Sp.

Small, elliptic. Striæ coarse, costate, 6 in 0,01 mm., reaching the median line, but abbreviated around the nodule.
Length 0,0375 mm. Breadth 0,0128 mm.
Pl. II, fig. 24, $^{1000}/_1$.
Balearic Islets (F. SÖDERLUND).

This small species seems to be the unnamed form in A. SCHMIDTS Atlas Pl. 46, fig. 7 and is perhaps according to GRUNOW the *N. mediterranea* KÜTZ. Bac. Pl. III, fig. XVII, which however is represented on much too small a scale to admet of identification. Another allied form is the yet unpublished *N. cotiformis* GRUN. from Demerara River, which has cuneate ends and 5 striæ in 0,01 mm. Length 0,06 mm. Breadth 0,014 mm.

16. *Navicula Anderssonii* CL. N. Sp.

Linear oblong, with almost cuneate ends. Striæ parallel or slightly radiate in the middle, $6^1/_2$—7 in 0,01 mm. not reaching the median line, which in surrounded by a narrow area, dilated around the central nodule.

Length 0,075 mm. Breadth 0,019 mm.

Pl. III, fig. 28, $^{1000}/_1$.

Gallapagos Islands (Eugenie Exp.).

I have named this species in honour of the late Prof. N. J. ANDERSSON, botanist to the Eugenie Expedition.

17. *Navicula marginulata* CL. N. Sp.

Rhombic; striæ very short, marginal, enclosing a large structureless area, 17 in 0,01 mm.

Length 0,042 mm. Breadth 0,012 mm.

Pl. III, fig. 29, $^{1000}/_1$.

Florida, near the Harbour of Pensacola, in a gathering sent by Mr. FEBIGER.

18. *Navicula (Powelli* LEWIS var.*) Gallapagensis* CL.

Linear oblong with cuneate ends. Striæ coarse, almost parallel, $8^1/_2$ in 0,01 mm., on both side of the median line interrupted by linear areas. There are thus four longitudinal series of short striæ, two near the margins and two close to the median line, interrupted near the central nodule.

Length 0,05—0,09 mm. Breadth 0,013—0,021 mm.

Gallapagos Islands (Eugenie Exp.).

Pl. III. fig. 30.

Of the true *N. Powellii* LEWIS I have not seen a figure, but GRUNOW states that his *N. Vidowichii* (Verh. 1863, Pl. IV, fig. 4) is the same species. I have seen the latter form in gatherings from Adriatic sea, kindly sent me by Mr. F. HAUCK, and I find that the form is different, the striæ more distant (6 in 0,01 mm.). Length 0,1122 mm. Breadth 0,02 mm. *N. Egyptiaca* GREV. Trans. Micr. Journ. XIV, p. 127, Pl. 12, fig. 16—17 seems to be the same, but the striæ are stated to be only 4 in 0,01 mm. Another allied form is, as far on may judge from the figure, *N. Zanardiniana* GRUN. (Verh. 1860, Pl. 3, fig. 12) with indistinctly punctate striæ, 6 in 0,01 mm., in four uninterrupted rows. Another, undescribed form is *N. Wittii* GRUN. Mspt. (Pl. III, fig. 31, $^{900}/_1$) from Brazil, which is not so long and slender as the last named species and has 8 striæ in 0,01 mm: The two following forms are also allied to *N. Powellii.*

19. *Navicula amica* CL. et GRUN.

Contracted in the middle, ends cuneate; striæ 7½ in 0,01 mm., almost parallel, smooth. The two interior rows of striæ are interrupted in the middle.
Length 0,075 mm. Breadth 0,023 mm.
Pl. III, fig. 37, $^{950}/_1$.
Tahiti (Eugenie Exp.).

20. *Navicula quadriseriata* CL. et GRUN.

Large, oblong oval with parallel sides and cuneate ends. Striæ smooth, 8 in 0,01 mm. in four longitudinal, uninterrupted rows. The interior striæ are shortened around the central nodule, which is surrounded by an orbicular area.
Length 0,09 mm. Breadth 0,035 mm.
Pl. III, fig. 32, $^{800}/_1$.
Balearic Islets very rare (F. SÖDERLUND).

Two other species, of which Mr. GRUNOW has sent me figures, seem to be related to the last described forms: *N. Castracanei* GRUN. (Pl. III, fig. 33, $^{900}/_1$) and *N. Petitiana* GRUN. (Pl. III, fig. 34, $^{900}/_1$). Both species are elliptic lanceolate and have the interior rows of striæ parallel with the margins of the valve, not close to the median line. *N. Castracanei* is 0,1 mm. in length, 0,03 mm. in breadth, and has 9 striæ in 0,01 mm. *N. Petitiana* is 0,07 mm. in length and 0,02 mm. in breadth and has 11 striæ in 0,01 mm.

All these species together with the following seem to form a section, for which Mr. GRUNOW has proposed (CL. et GRUN. Art. Diat. pag. 29), the name *quadri-seriatæ*:
This group contains:
Navicula Powellii LEWIS = N. Vidowichii GRUN.
N. Egyptiacæ GREV.
N. (Powellii var.) *Gallapagensis* CL.
N. Zanardiniana GRUN.
N. Wittii GRUN.
N. amica CL. et GRUN.
N. quadriseriata CL. et GRUN.
N. Castracanei GRUN.
N Petitiana GRUN.
? *N. (Stauroneis) robusta* PETIT (Diat. de l'île Campbell Pl. V, fig. 16).
N. biseriata PETIT (l. c. Pl. IV, fig. 15).
N. Richardsoniana O'MEARA (Irish Diat. Pl. 31, fig. 33).
N. Eugeniæ CL. (this paper pag. 7).
? *N. denticulata* O'MEARA (Quart. J. M. S. VII, p. 115, Pl. V, fig. 2, 1867).
? *N. Musca* EHB.
? *N. mirabilis* LEUDUGER FORTMOREL (Diat. de Ceylon Pl. II, fig. 21).
N. blanda A. SCHM. (Nordsee Diat. Pl. II, fig. 27).
N. latefasciata GRUN. (in CL. et GRUN. Arct. Diat. Pl. I, fig. 21).

N. subdivisa GRUN. (Nordsee Diat. fig. 20).
N. consimilis A. SCHM. (l. c. p. 46).
N. æmula GRUN. (in A. SCHM. Nordsee Diat. II, fig. 47).
N. superimposita A. SCHM. (Nordsee Diat. II, fig. 34 and Diat. Atl. Pl. 46, fig. 61).

To these species are two undescribed forms nearly allied: *N. Bruchii* GRUN. and *N. multiseriata* GRUN.

N. Bruchii GRUN. (Pl. III. fig. 35, $^{900}/_1$) found on Tahiti, is in length 0,04 mm. and in breadth 0,012 mm.

N. multiseriata GRUN. (Pl. III, fig. 36, $^{900}/_1$) from Tongatabu, is in length 0,036.

Navicula. Section: Pseudo-amphiprora CL.

I propose to include in this section a small number of Navicula-forms, which are in some respects akin to Amphiprora and in other to Stauroneis. The valve on both sides in the median line is divided by a keel into two portions. The central nodule is transversely dilated into a short stauros, reaching the above named keels. The type of the section is:

Navicula arctica CL.

In my paper On the arctic Diat. (Bih. till K. Sv. Vet. Ak. Handl. 1873, 1, N:o 13, p. 16, Pl. III, fig. 13).

This fine species was first described and somewhat indifferently figured by BAILAY (SMITHS. Contr. Vol. VII, p. 8. fig. 14 and 15, 1853) as *Amphora stauroptera*. GREGORY afterwards gave (in his Diat. of Clyde 1857, p. 34, Pl. IV, fig. 59 c.) a very fine figure of the species in question in S. V., but he regardes it as *Amphiprora lepidoptera*. At the same time he describes the F. V. as *Amph. obtusa* (fig. 60 l. c.). but Mr. LAGERSTEDT (Bih. till K. Sv. Vet. Ak. Handl. T. III, N:o 15, p. 46) has found that the two figures (59 and 60) belong to the same species. As the names N. stauroptera and N. obtusa have been used for other forms it will be most conveniant to name the species N. arctica. A. SCHMIDT has figured the species in his Nordsee Diat. Pl. III, fig. 1 as *Amphiprora obtusa* GREG. If the *Nav. arctica* O'MEARA (Micr. Journ. Vol. XIV, Pl. VIII, fig. 1) belongs to this species I d'ont know.

The Nav. arctica lives in the northern part of the Atlantic. It has been issued in CL. et MÖLL. Diat. N:o 57.

21. *Navicula jugata* CL.

Elegantly elliptic with parallel, indistinct, and punctate striæ, 10 in 0,01 mm., between the keels and the margins. The median portion of the valve, between the keels, seems in very oblique light and with good objectives to be exceedingly finely striate.

Length 0,093 mm. Breadth 0,024 mm.
Pl. III, fig. 38, $^{300}/_1$.
Gallapagos Islands rare (Eugenie Exp.).

GRUNOW has found in the Campeche Bay gathering a closely allied form, *Amphiprora Campechiana* GRUN. (Arct. Diat. pag. 66), which has $12^1/_2$ striæ in 0,01 mm. and another species with 15 striæ in 0,01 mm. and obtuse ends.

22. *Navicula Pensacolæ* CL. N. Sp.

Lanceolate, with undulate margins and prominent apices. Striæ indistinct, punctate, 15 in 0,01 mm., parallel. The portion of the valve between the keels is very indistinctly striate.

Length 0,054 mm. Breadth 0,015 mm.
Pl. III, fig. 39, $^{1000}/_1$.

Florida near the Harbour of Pensacola in a gathering sent by Mr. FEBIGER.

The following species is perhaps related to the species of this section:

23. *Navicula Gallapagensis* CL. N. Sp.

Panduriform, with cuneate ends. Striæ transverse, parallel, 15 in 0,01 mm., indistinctly punctate, reaching the median line and interrupted by a line or keel. The median part of the valve around the median line is striate.

Length 0,067—0,092 mm. Breadth 0,025 mm.
Pl. III, fig. 40, $^{850}/_1$ a. S. V. b. F. V.

Gallapagos Islands rare (Eugenie Exp.).

Stauroneis EHR.

1. *Stauroneis Balearica* CL. N. Sp.

Elongated, with acute ends. Stauros very short. Striæ transverse, 26 in 0,01 mm., and longitudinal 23 in 0,01 mm., crossing each other in right angles.

Length 0,11 mm. Breadth 0,013 mm.
Pl. III, fig. 41, a. $^{600}/_1$, b. structure $^{2000}/_1$.

Balearic Islets rare (F. SÖDERLUND).

This species is nearly akin to *St. Quarnerensis* (GRUN. in litt.) from the Adriatic Sea, which has also a short stauros and 18 longitudinal striæ in 0,01 mm.

2. *Stauroneis sulcata* CL. N. Sp.

Linear, with cuneate ends, stauros reaching the margin. Structure: strong, longitudinal lines or furrows, parallel with the median line, and transverse parallel striæ, 21 in 0,01 mm.

Length 0,088—0,109 mm. Breadth 0,008—0,009 mm.
Pl. III, fig. 46, $^{1000}/_1$.
Balearic Islets rare (F. SÖDERLUND).

Among the Stauroneis forms, known to me, there are two, which have a similar structure: *St. Stodderi* LEWIS and *St. Stodderi* var. *insignis* GRUN., both freshwater species. *St. sulcata* is marine and has finer striæ.

3. *Stauroneis Africana* CL. N. Sp.

Valve very convex, hyaline, elongate. Stauros reaching the margins. Striæ fine, 23 in 0,01 mm., parallel, reaching the median line.

Length 0,05 mm. Breadth 0,01 mm.
Pl. III, fig. 42, $^{1000}/_1$, a. F.V., b. S.V.

Fresh, or very slightly brackish water, Zwathrops River, Port Elisabeth, South Africa in a sample sent by Mr. W. JOSHUA (CL. and MÖLL. Diat. N:o 196).

This form is nearly related to *S. salina* W. SM., but has finer striæ. The striæ of *S. salina* are 17 in 0,01 mm.

4. *Stauroneis pachycephala* CL. N. Sp.

Linear, gibbous in the middle and at the ends, which are broadly rounded and capitate. Striæ oblique, very fine, about 29 in 0,01 mm., reaching the median line. Stauros reaching the margin. Median line straight. Terminal nodules turned in opposite direction.

Length 0,055 mm. Breadth 0,009 mm.
Pl. III, fig. 43, $^{1000}/_1$.

Fresh or slightly brackish water, Baakens River, Port Elizabeth, South Africa in a sample sent by Mr. JOSHUA (CL. et MÖLL. N:o 197).

This species comes nearest to *St. desiderata* CL. (in CL. et GRUN. Arctische Diat. Pl. III, fig. 58), which also has the terminal nodules turned in opposite direction, but the outline of this species is different and its striæ are almost parallel and much coarser. Both belong to a section parallel with GRUNOWS section Pseudopleurosigma of Navicula.

5. *Stauroneis (Pleurostauron) Sagitta* CL. N. Sp.

Elongated, apiculate, to the outline resembling *St. Smithii* GRUN. Ends with short interior diaphrams as in Pleurostauron. Striæ oblique 21 in 0,01 mm. one or two in the middle very strong.

Length 0,03—0,04 mm. Breadth 0,006—0,01 mm.
Pl. III, fig. 45, $^{1000}/_1$.

Fresh water, mouth of Tana Elf, Finmarken, collected by Prof. TH. M. FRIES (CL. et MÖLL. Diat. N:o 261 not rare).

This form has the appearance of *S. Smithii* GRUN., but is larger and has coarser striæ (being 28 in 0,01 mm. on S. Smithii) not so parallel as in *S. Smithii*.

Schizostauron GRUN.

1. *Schizostauron Crucicula* GRUN.

Striæ oblique, fine, 25 in 0,01 mm. Stauros bifid with very divergent branches, reaching the margins.
Length 0.03 mm. Breadth 0,009 mm.
Pl. III, fig. 44, $^{1000}/_1$.
Merrimac River U. St. on Chara, very rare in a gathering sent by Mr. O. NORDSTEDT.[1])

Nitzschia W. SM.

1. *Nitzschia ocellata* CL.

This species has already been described in CL. et GRUN. Arct. Diat. p. 80. The frustule is panduriform; the keel central with 8—10 puncta in 0,01 mm. The striæ are fine, 22 in 0,01 mm. composed of small, elongate puncta. The striæ are sharper and more distant in the centre of the valve. The whole valve is covered with large scattered puncta sometimes arranged in irregular, transverse lines.

Length 0,08—0,1 mm. Breadth of the frustule 0,027 mm. at the constriction 0.018 mm.
Pl. IV. fig. 47, $^{1000}/_1$, *a*. valve. *b*. frustle.
Balearic Islets (Dr. SÖDERLUND). CL. et MÖLL. Diat. N:o 154—155 rare.

This species is placed by GRUNOW in his section Pseudoamphiprora, very nearly to Perrya KITTON.

2. *Nitzschia prælonga* CL.

This species has already been described in CL. et GRUN. Arct. Diat. p. 85. The frustules are extremely long and slender, slightly arcuate, linear, with obliquely cuneate ends. Keel almost central, with about 5 puncta in 0,01 mm. The striæ are strong, 16 in 0,01 mm.

Length 0,25 mm. Breadth 0,009 mm.
Pl. IV, fig. 48, *a*. $^{600}/_1$. *b*. $^{1000}/_1$.
Balearic Islets not rare (Dr. F. SÖDERLUND).

[1]) In printing this paper I have been informed by Mr. GRUNOW that he has found the same form abundantly in pools of the Rio Purus, Brazil, and that he has named it in Linnæan Society Journ. of May 1880 I consequently adopt his name.

Surirella Turpin.

1. *Surirella Caldensis* Cl. N. Sp.
Very long and slender, linear, with cuneate ends. Alæ high. Canaliculi short, numerous, 4—5 in 0,01 mm. Margin striate; striæ punctate 20 in 0,01 mm. F. V. linear, not cuneate.
Length 0,108 mm. Breadth 0,013 mm.
Pl. IV, fig. 50, $^{1000}/_1$.
Brazil, Caldas on Sphagnum (Dr. Hj. Mosén). Cl. et Möll. Diat. N:o 212, common.
This species comes near to *S. arcta* A. Schm. Atl. Pl. 23, fig. 23—24 from Demerara, but its canaliculi are shorter and denser.

2. *Surirella degenerans* Cl. N. Sp.
Oblong, with very broad ends and slightly contracted middle. Margins striate. Costæ obsolete, consisting only of the dilated portion. Area with some scattered markings and striæ.
Length 0,09—0,072 mm. Breadth 0,037—0,046 mm.
Pl. IV, fig. 51, $^{500}/_1$.
Gallapagos Islands (Eugenie Exp.).
This form, which belongs to the variable section of *S. lata*, is related to *S. laxa* Janisch.

3. *Surirella formosa* Cl. N. Sp.
Panduriform with large, rounded ends. Margin striate. Costæ abbreviate, with the dilated portion comparatively large. The middle of the valve is occupied by a narrow linear area, defined by short striæ.
Length 0,22 mm. Breadth 0,11 mm. at the constriction 0,07 mm.
Pl. IV, fig. 49, $^{500}/_1$.
Gallapagos Islands extremely rare (Eugenie Exp.).
This very large and beautiful Surirella does not agree with any of the many forms belonging to *S. lata*-section hitherto figured.

Campylodiscus Ehb.

1. *Campylodiscus (Ecclesianus* var.?) *peramplus* Cl.
Very large, costæ numerous 4—5 in 0,01 mm., equal in length, marginal. Area large with a circle of puncta and with some stellate markings.
Diam. 0,12—0,16 mm.
Pl. IV, fig. 53, $^{600}/_1$.
Gallapagos Islands (Eugenie Exp.).

The *C. Ecclesianus* Grev. (1857) is as Mr. Janisch correctly states the same as *C. fenestratus* Grev., which is the entire frustule. Mr. Janisch proposed (1863) the name *C. Rabenhorstianus*, but which should be changed for the older name of Greville's. The type of this extremely variable species, especially abundant in the caribbean area, has alternating longer and shorter costæ and an area not surrounded by a circlet of puncta. The form from Gallapagos Islands is therefore distinct, but, considering the great variability of the species, I am inclined to regard it only as a variety.

The stellate markings on the disc are very variable, and in some specimens wanting.

2. *Campylodiscus Margaritarum* Cl. N. Sp.

Costæ numerous, covering about $^2/_3$ of the disc, interrupted by a fine line and surrounding an elongate area, where some fragmentary punctate lines are visible as the continuation of the costæ.

Diam. 0,06 mm.

Pl. IV, fig. 52, $^{500}/_1$.

Pearl Islands rare (Eugenie Exp.).

In its general form this species resembles *C. angularis* Grev., but is different.

Plagiogramma Grev.

1. *Plagiogramma rutilarioides* Cl. N. Sp.

Small, rhombic, more or less elongate, with two converging costæ around the centre, but not near the ends. Structure: transverse punctate lines, 15 in 0,01 mm. Margin with one or two sets of larger puncta, which probably are the bases of bristles.

Length 0,03—0,0425 mm. Breadth 0,01—0,013 mm.

Pl. IV, fig. 54, $^{1000}/_1$.

Port Jackson, Australia (Eugenie Exp.).

2. *Plagiogramma spinosum* Cl. N. Sp.

Valve narrow, constricted in the middle, then dilated, and again constricted. Costæ 2 strong, around the centre. Ends slightly capitate. Structure: puncta, arranged in regular transverse rows, 10 in 0,01 mm. and in irregular longitudinal lines. The margin of the frustule is furnished with a row of short setæ or bristles. The ends of the valves have blank (not punctate), oval areas.

Length 0,08 mm. Breadth 0,01 mm.

Pl. IV, fig. 55, $^{900}/_1$.

The marginal setæ are visible when the frustule lies in an oblique position.

Gallapagos Islands rare (Eugenie Exp.).

This form has the same general outline as *P. caribbæum* Cl., *P. lyratum* Grev and *P. Barbadense* Grev. It is most nearly akin to the latter, but the ends are dissimilar and the structure different.

Rutilaria Grev.

1. *Rutilaria recens* Cl. N. Sp.

Valve plane, elliptic or elongate with acute ends. It is covered with numerous scattered puncta, which sometimes are arranged in irregular lines. Besides these there are in the centre of the valve some more strongly marked puncta, and which seem to belong to another stratum of the valve. The margin has a row of puncta, which are, as may be seen in the F. V., short spines. In the F. V. the ends of the valve terminate in short processes.

Length 0,037—0,11 mm. Breadth 0,02 mm.

Pl. IV, fig. 57, a. $^{1000}/_1$ (an abnorm specimen having no puncta on a part of the valve), b. $^{800}/_1$ small specimen.

Gallapagos Islands (Eugenie Exp.).

The genus Rutilaria established by Dr. Greville, comprises only some few species, all fossil. These are *R. Epsilon* Grev., rare in Monterey stone, *R. superba* (and var.? *ventricosa*) Grev. and *R. elliptica* Grev. from Barbados. They all have the curious markings in the centre of the valve, which are elevations above the level of the frustule, as is visible on the fig. 10, Pl. XI, T. Micr. Soc. Vol. XIV. In our recent species these markings are represented only by the strongly marked puncta. From Greville's fig. of the F. V. of *R. elliptica* and *R. superba* it is evident that the valve is plane and that its apices are produced into processes, and farther that the margins of the frustule are bounded with a row af setæ, exactly as in our species.

The position of Rutilaria is somewhat uncertain. Greville has pointed out its relationship to Nitzschia and Fragilarieæ. Prof. Hamilton Smith places it among the Melosiræ. It has however no real affinity with Nitzschia or Melosiræ, but is very nearly allied to the genus *Cymatosira* Grun., of which the only known species *C. Lorenziana* Grun. has also marginal bristles. The Cymatosira is without doubt nearly related to Dimerogramma.

Mr. Kitton writes to me in a letter about a new species of Rutilaria from the Californian deposits, *Rut. obesum* Grev. Mpt. The valve has 3 inflations, the central being the largest; the apices are shortly cuneate; one third of the area is smooth, the remainder distinctly covered with irregular markings. The central nodule consists of a nebulous circular spot, upon which is placed a short spiral (?) ring. Margin distinctly punctate. Mr. Kitton has seen about half a dozen specimens of this species, all frustles, and in no case was he able to separate the valves. I crushing partially one specimen in balsam, he observed that the nebulous central nodule was the base of a siliceous isthmus, connecting the two valves.

Actinella LEWIS.

1. *Actinella Guianensis* GRUN. in litt.

Of the genus Actinella only one species, the *A. punctata* LEWIS from White Mountain Deposits, is known. The genus, which is nearly related to Eunotia, is distinguished by the different development of the ends. The puncta, which follow the margins of A. punctata as well as of A. Guianensis, are also visible in true Eunotia, for instance *E. denticulata* BRÉB.

The Actinella Guianensis, which occurs rarely in CL. et MÖLL. Diat. N:o 212, is larger than *A. punctata* and has 14—16 striæ in 0,01 mm., varying in different parts of the valve.

Length of frustule 0,105 mm. Breadth of one end 0,007 of the other 0,011 mm.
Pl. V, fig. 58, $^{1000}/_1$.

Brazil, Caldas on mosses (Dr. HJ. MOSÉN).

Asterolampra EHB.

1. *Asterolampra Balearica* CL. N. Sp.

Rays about 10, not reaching the margin of the disc. Umbilicus small, the diameter being only $^1/_4$—$^1/_5$ of that of the disc. Umbilical rays are straight and not branched. The compartments are covered by cellules arranged into lines, crossing each other in three directions, 9 in 0,01 mm.

Diameter of the valve 0,0715 mm.

Balearic Islets extremely rare (F. SÖDERLUND).

Pl. V, fig. 59, *a*. $^{470}/_1$, *b*. a compartment $^{1000}/_1$.

This species appears to be related to *Asterolampra Grevillei* WALLICH, which also occurs in the Balearic gathering, but this species has much finer cellulation (20—22 lines in 0,01 mm.). The *A. centraster* JOHNST. Micr. Journ. VIII, p. 12, Pl. I, fig. 10 is more nearly related, but its umbilicus is larger.

Coscinodiscus EHB.

1. *Coscinodiscus undulatus* CL. N. Sp.

The surface of the disc elevated in the middle and with an elevated ring halfway between the centre and the margin. Surface covered with dense, pearllike puncta arranged in lines radiating from the centre to the margin, where they become smaller, much more crowded and form short striæ.

Diam. 0,096 mm.

Pl. V, fig. 60, *a*. $^{450}/_1$, *b*. $^{300}/_1$ outline of a valve in oblique position.

Melosira Ag.

1. *Melosira (Podosira?) tuberculosa* Cl. N. Sp.

Frustule perfectly sphærical, with very narrow connecting membrane, which forms merely an equatorial line. Valve irregularly covered with scattered tubercules. With good lenses the surface between the tubercules is seen to be covered with fine striæ, 20 in 0,01 mm., crossing each other at an angle of 60°.

Diam. 0,05 mm.
Pl. V, fig. 65, $^{600}/_1$.

Gallapagos Islands rare (Eugenie Exp.).

Stictodiscus Grev.

1. *Stictodiscus Novaræ* Cl. N. Sp.

Disc circular, with irregularly scattered large puncta in the centre. Radiating lines few. Between each pair of these lines there are about 6 rows of tolerably large puncta. Margin of the disc striate.

Diam. 0,15 mm.
Pl. V, fig. 66, $^{570}/_1$.

Fossil, Nankoori Deposit (Novara Expedition) in a sample communicated by Mr. Grunow, rare.

I first supposed this elegant form to be a variety of *Stictodiscus Crozieri* Kitton (Micr. Journ. 1873, Pl. 38, fig. 2) but on comparing my specimen with a specimen of *S. Crozieri*, I found too great a difference. The puncta are much larger and the radiate lines not so numerous as in *S. Crozieri*. Besides the margin in striate.

Stephanodiscus Ehr.

1. *Stephanodiscus (bellus* A. Schm. var.?) *Novæ Zeelandiæ* Cl.

This beautiful little disc has about 20 radiate costæ, bifurcate near the margin, where no spines are visible. The whole surface is covered with small puncta, arranged in lines, radiating from the irregularly punctate centre. Two such punctate lines fill the space between each pair of costæ.

Diam. 0,02—0,03 mm.

New Zeeland, fresh or very slightly brackish water, Rotorua Lake, in some samples communicated by Dr. S. Berggren.

Pl. V, fig. 62, $^{1000}/_1$.

The *Cyclotella bella* A. Schm. Nordsee Diat. p. 94, Pl. 3, fig. 39 is a small marine species, which seems to correspond in all essential characters with the New Zeeland specimens.

Cyclotella Kütz.

1. *Cyclotella Meneghiniana* var.? *stelligera* Cl. et Grun.

Disc with marginal striæ, about 14 in 0,01 mm., and with a central star of radiating lines, alternately shorter and larger.

Diam. 0,022 mm.

Pl. V, fig. 63, $^{1000}/_1$. *a*. Specim. from New Zeeland; *c*. small specimen from Lac de Gerardmer (Vosgues).

New Zeeland, Rotorua Lake, coll. by S. Berggren.

Another variety *stellulifera* Grun. is represented by the fig. *b*. and is characterized by the granulate striæ.

Liradiscus Grev.

1. *Liradiscus* (?) *Capensis* Cl. N. Sp.

Circular, with a narrow, striate margin (with 15 striæ in 0,01 mm.). Disc covered with curved and branching, but not anastomosing lines or markings, which do not form a coherent network.

Diam. 0,04 mm.

Pl. V, fig. 61, $^{700}/_1$.

Marine, Cape of Good Hope in a slide sent by Mr. F. Hauck.

Of the genus Liradiscus only four species are known, all fossil from Barbados deposit. Our form, if it really belongs to Liradiscus, is the first known as recent. It is doubtful if it not would be better to place it in Cyclotella, as it has some relationship to *C. striata* Kütz. or *C. Dallasiana*.

Auliscus Bail.

1. *Auliscus* (?) *insignis* Cl. N. Sp.

Disc almost orbicular with 2 rounded, not truncate processes, and divided by a large cruciform blank area in to four compartments. The compartments have a very singular structure and seem to be covered with irregular depressions. In the F. V. they are elevated and the processes rounded.

Diam. 0,12 mm.

Pl. V, fig. 64, *a*. $^{800}/_1$, S. V. *b*. $^{300}/_1$, F. V.

Gallapagos Island extremely rare (Eugenie Exp.).

I am unacquainted with any Auliscus having the rounded processes of this glorious species; it should perhaps be placed in the genus Cerataulus.

Annother remarkable species of Auliscus (*A. Ralfsianus* Grev.) hitherto known only in a fossil state from the Barbados Deposit, occurs in the extremely interesting Gallapagos material.

Biddulphia GRAY.

1. *Biddulphia Moronensis* CL. N. Sp.

Valve in S. V. oval, stout, with two strong transverse costæ and two large and stout oval processes. Structure: large, irregularly scattered puncta on the valve and fine dots arranged in irregular lines on the processes.

Length of the valve 0,12 mm. Breadth 0,07 mm.

Pl. IV, fig. 56, $^{500}/_1$.

Moron deposit in a slide from Mr. J. D. MÖLLER.

2. *Biddulphia tentaculifera* CL. N. Sp.

Valve elevate, covered with tolerably large puncta arranged irregular lines around the centre of the valve. No costæ are visible. Processes elongate, club shaped.

Diam. of the valve 0,05 mm.

Pl. V, fig. 67, $^{800}/_1$.

Keeling Island (Eugenie Exp.).

3. *Biddulphia Gallapagensis* CL. N. Sp.

S. V. broadly oval, almost orbicular, with two short stout processes. Structure: pearly granules arranged in lines, radiating from the irregularly punctate centre to the margin, about 12—13 in 0,01 mm.

Longest diameter 0,049 mm., shortest 0,04 mm.

Pl. VI, fig. 74, $^{1000}/_1$.

Gallapagos Islands (Eugenie Exp.).

This form belongs to the section of *B. aurita*, which contains a large number of nearly allied forms, as *B. Roperiana*, *B. Edwardii* FEBIGER etc.

Triceratium EHB.

1. *Triceratium (Hydrosera; Terpsinoe?) trifoliatum* CL. N. Sp.

Valve plane, with concave sides and three 3-cuspidate angles, separated from the valve by transverse lines (incomplete diaphragms). Surface covered with small puncta arranged in irregular lines.

Diam. 0,045 mm. Distance between two apices 0,05—0,06 mm.

Pl. VI, fig. 71, $^{600}/_1$.

New Zeeland in fresh or slightly brackish water collected by Mr. S. BERGGREN very rare.

This curious species is remarkable for its freshwater habit and seems to be most nearly related to Hydrosera *Wallich* from the Ganges, but it is entirely different.

2. *Triceratium (Hydrosera; Terpsinoë) Javanicum* CL. N. Sp.

Valve plane, hexagonal, with three angles separated from the disc by transverse lines (diaphragms) and alternating with three other angles, which are contiguous with the disc. One of the three latter angles has near the apex a small transvere fissure corresponding to the appendages on *Hydrosera triquetra* WALLICH. Structure irregular 5—7-gonal cells, 4—5 in 0,01 mm., absent from the ends of the three first named angles. F. W. Rectangular with longitudinal furrows, corresponding to the sinuses between the angles.

Diam. 0,075 mm.

Pl. VI, fig. 75, $^{600}/_1$.

Java, Batavia in brackish water (Eugenie Exp.).

This form is so nearly related to Hydrosera triquetra WALLICH Micr. Journ. VI, p. 251, Pl. 13, fig. 1—6, that it perhaps might be more correctly regarded as a mere variety.

3. *Triceratium dubium* BTW.

Micr. Journ. VII, p. 180, Pl. 9, fig. 12 is the triangular form of *T. bicorne* CL. (Bih. t. K. Sv. Vet.-Ak Handl. Pl. 5, fig. 30).

4. *Triceratium Tripos* CL. N. Sp.

Outline in the S. V. almost orbicular or triangular with very broad and rounded angles. Processes three near the angles. Structure a somewhat coarse and irregular cellulation of hexagonal cells, about 5 in 0,01 mm. In the F. V. the valve is elevated, sloping regularly from the apex to the margins. The three processes are strong and and project somewhat obliquely.

Diam. of the valve 0,0525 mm.

Pl. VI, fig. 72, $^{900}/_1$.

Gallapagos Islands (Eugenie Exp.).

5. *Triceratium Anderssonii* CL. N. Sp.

This very rare and exceedingly fine species, of which I have found only one incomplete specimen, is quadrangular with straight sides and rounded angles, upon which are large truncate processes. The structure consists of branching veins, radiating from the centre to the margins, and of tolerably coarse cellules, about 5 in 0,01 mm., of which two rows fill the space between each pair of lines.

Greatest diameter 0,09 mm.

Pl. VI, fig. 69, $^{500}/_1$.

Gallapagos Islands (Eugenie Exp.).

The structure of this remarkable species, which I have named in honour of the late Prof. N. J. ANDERSSON, is that of a Stictodiscus.

6. **Triceratium læve** Cl. N. Sp.

Triangular or quadratic, with straight sides and acute not produced angles. The surface perfectly smooth, no structure being visible on balsam-specimens. In F. V. the centre of the valve is elevated, and the angles are produced into processes, forming right angles with the transverse diameter.

Distance between angles 0,02—0,0285 mm.

Pl. VI, fig. 70, $^{100}/_1$, a. S. V., b. F. V.

Gallapagos Islands (Eugenie Exp.).

7. **Triceratium (productum** Grev. var.) **Balearicum** Cl. et Grun. (in Cl. et Möll. Diat. N:o 154—155).

This form is closely allied to *Amphitetras producta* Greville and *Triceratium Antillarum* Cl. Its outline is 4—5 angular, with the angles produced into short processes. The centre of the valve is elevated and by a depression separated from the margins. The structure consists of rounded puncta arranged in lines, radiating from the centre to the angles, about 5 in 0,01 mm.

Greatest diameter 0,06—0,08 mm.

Pl. VI, fig. 73, $^{500}/_1$.

Balearic Islets (Dr. F. Söderlund).

There can be not doubt that *A. producta* Grev. (Micr. Journ. II, p. 94, Pl. 9, fig. 2) and *T. Antillarum* Cl. (Bih. till K. Sv. Vet.-Ak. Handl. Bd. V, N:o 8, Pl. V, fig. 29) belong to the same species, which seems to be nearly allied also to *Amphitetras elegans* Grev. from Monterey stone, in which form the depression between the centre and the margins form an inscribed quadrate.

Allied to these forms seems to be *Am. nobilis* Grev. (Trans. Micr. Soc. 1865, p. 105, Pl. IX, fig. 27) from the Red Sea. This species is however larger and seems to be only the pentagonal form of *Am. antediluviana*. It occurs in Rabenhorst, Alg. Eur. N:o 2264 from Livorno together with Am. antediluviana, and Mr. Kitton informs me that he has found it in samples from Orkney Islands and Southampton; he also remarks that the processes are much exaggerated in Grevilles figure. Another form related to A. antediluviana is *A. tessellata* Shadb. (T. M. S. 1854, p. 16, Pl. 1, fig. 11), of which a variety with very coarse cellulation and large processes occurs in Moron Deposit.

The *Triceratium productum* Grev. from Barbados Deposit is a quite different form (see T. M. S. 1863, IX, p. 69, Pl. VIII, fig. 9).

8. **Triceratium Gallapagense** Cl. N. Sp.

Triangular, with acute angles, not provided with processes. Structure: distant puncta, scattered over the disc of the valve, closer near the margins, where they form

short rows, 5 in 0,01 mm. In the angles the puncta are much smaller and form fine branching lines.
Distance between angles 0,0975 mm.
Pl. VI, fig. 72, $^{600}/_1$.
Gallapagos Islands rare (Eugenie Exp.).

9. *Triceratium margaritiferum* Cl. N. Sp.
Valve quadrangular with concave sides and rounded angles, without processes. Surface probably plane. Structure tolerably coarse granules arranged near the margins in short lines, smaller in the angles, rare and scattered in the middle.
Diam. 0,05 mm.
Pl. VI, fig. 76, $^{600}/_1$.
Gallapagos Islands rare (Eugenie Exp.).

Chætoceros Ehr.

1. *Chætoceros Dichæta* Ehr. = *C. remotus* Cl. et Grun.
This form has already been described in Cl. et Grun. Arct. Diat. p. 119 and is to be found in most slides of Cl. et Möll. Diat. N:o 125.
Pl. VI, fig. 77, $^{600}/_1$.
Antarctic Ocean (Challenger Exp.).

Rhizosolenia Ehr.

1. *Rhizosolenia (alata* var.?) *gracillima* Cl..
Extremely long and slender, measuring 0,5—0,7 mm. in length and only 0,006 mm. in breadth. The beaks are almost straight, provided with pocket-like impressions. The zig-zag markings on the connecting membrane are very indistinct. The frustule is extremely hyaline, having no colour in dry state. No structure has been seen.
Pl. VI, fig. 78, $^{1000}/_1$.
West coast of Sweeden, Lysekil, freely floting on the surface of the sea (July 1877 by P. T. Cleve).

Another slender species, characterized by its coarse, of puncta composed striæ, *Rh. Shrubsolii* Cl. N. Sp., occurs in the Atlantic Ocean between Iceland and Greenland. It was recently found in great abundance on the surface of the sea near the island of Sheppey by Mr. Shrubsole.

Description of plates I—VI.

Plate I.

Fig. 1. Mastogloia panduriformis Cl.
» 2. M. submarginata Cl. et Grun.
» 3. Amphora Berggrenii Cl.
» 4. Cymbella Brasiliana Cl.
» 5. C. Stodderi Cl.
» 6. Pleurosigma tortuosum Cl.
» 7. Pl. lanceolatum var. cuspidatum Cl.
» 8. Pl. (Donkinia?) longissimum Cl.
» 9. Rhoicosigma mediterraneum Cl.
» 10. Navicula (Fluminensis var.?) Floridana Cl.
» 11. N. cruciata Cl.
» 12. N. Platessa Cl.
» 13. N. Grœnlandica Cl.
» 14. N. Hennedyi var. Tahitensis Cl.
» 15. N. Hennedyi var. minuta Cl.

Plate II.

Fig. 16. Navicula Eugeniæ Cl.
» 17. N. rudis Cl.
» 18. N. Holmiensis Cl.
» 19. N. Hennedyi var. undulata Cl.
» 20. N. (excavata var.?) Angelorum Cl.
» 21. N. Febigerii Cl.
» 22. N. Cluthensis var. minuta Cl.
» 23. N. Cluthensis var.? maculifera Cl.
» 24. N. Fromenteræ Cl.
» 25. N. bicuspidata Cl. et Grun.
» 26. N. mesoleia Cl.
» 27. N. Hauckii Cl

Plate III.

Fig. 28. Navicula Anderssonii Cl.
» 29. N. marginulata Cl.
» 30. N. Powellii Lewis var. Gallapagensis Cl.
» 31. N. Wittii Grun.*
» 32. N. quadriserieta Cl. et Grun.
» 33. N. Castracanei Grun.*
» 34. N. Petitiana Grun.*
» 35. N. Bruchii Grun.*

*) Delineated by Mr. Grunow.

Fig. 36. Navicula multiseriata GRUN. *
» 37. N. amica CL. et GRUN.
» 38. N. jugata CL.
» 39. N. Pensacola CL.
» 40. N. Gallapagensis CL.
» 41. Stauroneis Balearica CL.
» 42. St. Africana CL.
» 43. St. pachycephala CL.
» 44. Schizostauron Crucicula GRUN.
» 45. Stauroneis Sagitta CL.
» 46. St. sulcata CL.

Plate IV.

Fig. 47. Nitzschia ocellata CL.
» 48. N. prælonga CL.
» 49. Surirella formosa CL.
» 50. S. Caldensis CL.
» 51. S. degenerans CL.
» 52. Campylodiscus Margaritarum CL.
» 53. C. (Ecclesianus var.?) peramplus CL.
» 54. Plagiogramma rutilarioides CL.
» 55. P. spinosum CL.
» 56. Biddulphia Moroneusis CL.
» 57. Rutilaria recens CL.

Plate V.

Fig. 58. Actinella Guianensis GRUN.
» 59. Asterolampra Balearica CL.
» 60. Coscinodiscus undulatus CL.
» 61. Liradiscus Capensis CL.
» 62. Stephanodiscus (bellus var.?) Novæ Zeelandiæ CL.
» 63. Cyclotella Meneghiniana var. stelligera CL. et GRUN. a. from New Zeeland; b. from France; c. stellulifera GRUN.
» 64. Auliscus (?) insignis CL.
» 65. Melosira (Podosira?) tuberculosa CL.
» 66. Stictodiscus Novaræ CL.
» 67. Biddulphia tentaculifera CL.

Plate VI.

Fig. 68. Triceratium Tripos CL.
» 69. T. Anderssonii CL.
» 70. T. læve CL.
» 71. T. (Terpsinoe?) trifoliatum CL.
» 72. T. Gallapagense CL.
» 73. T. productum GREV. var. Balearicum CL. et GRUN.
» 74. Biddulphia Gallapagensis CL.
» 75. Triceratium (Terpsinoe?) Javanicum CL
» 76. T. margaritiferum CL.
» 77. Chætoceros Dichæta EHR.
» 78. Rhizosolenia (alata var.?) gracillima CL.

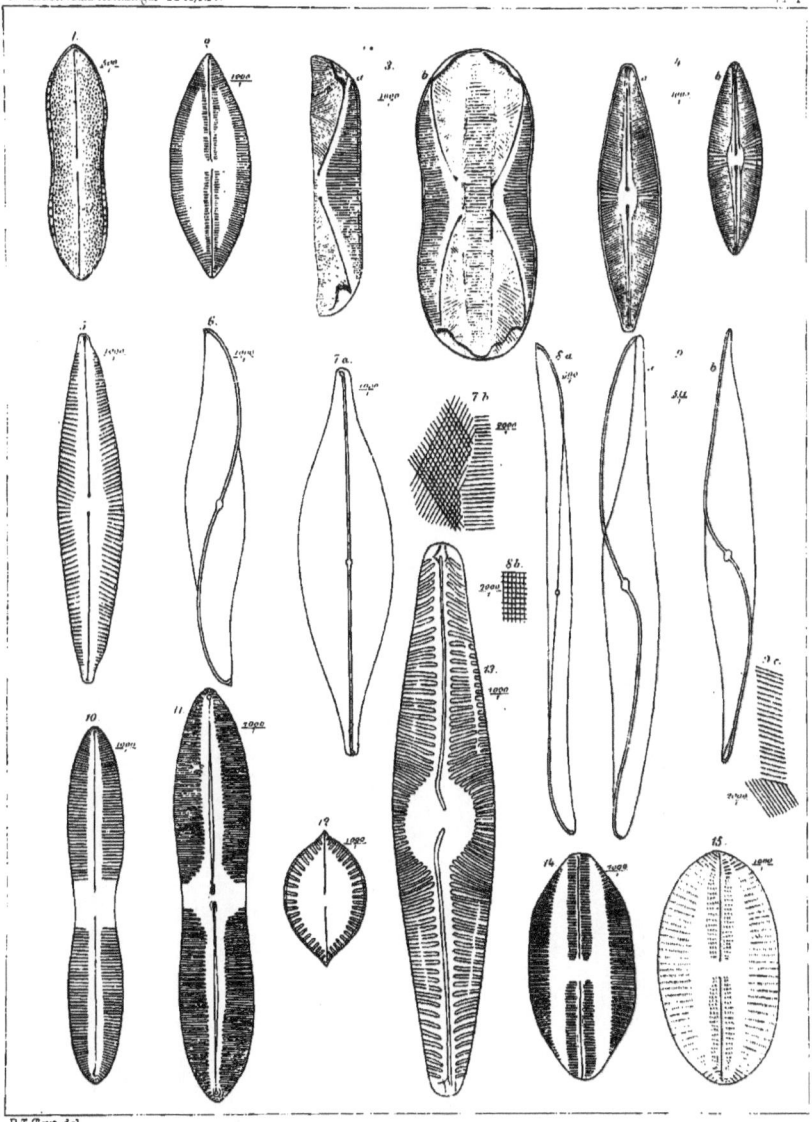

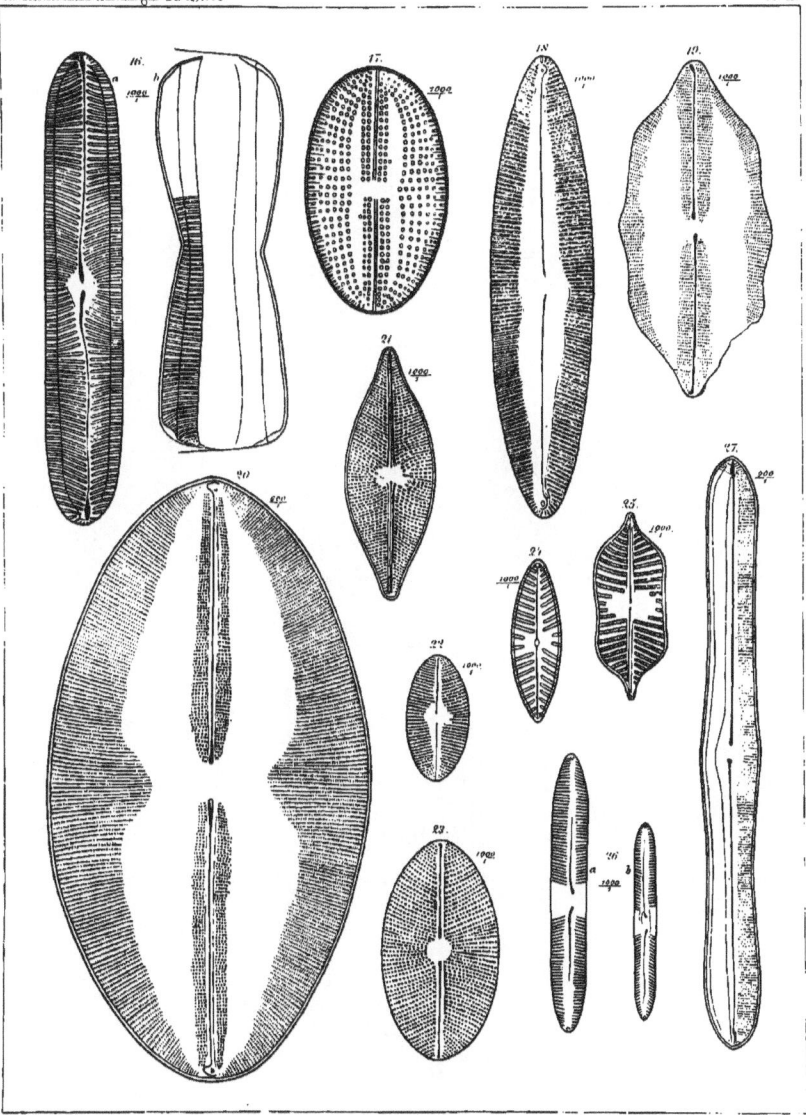

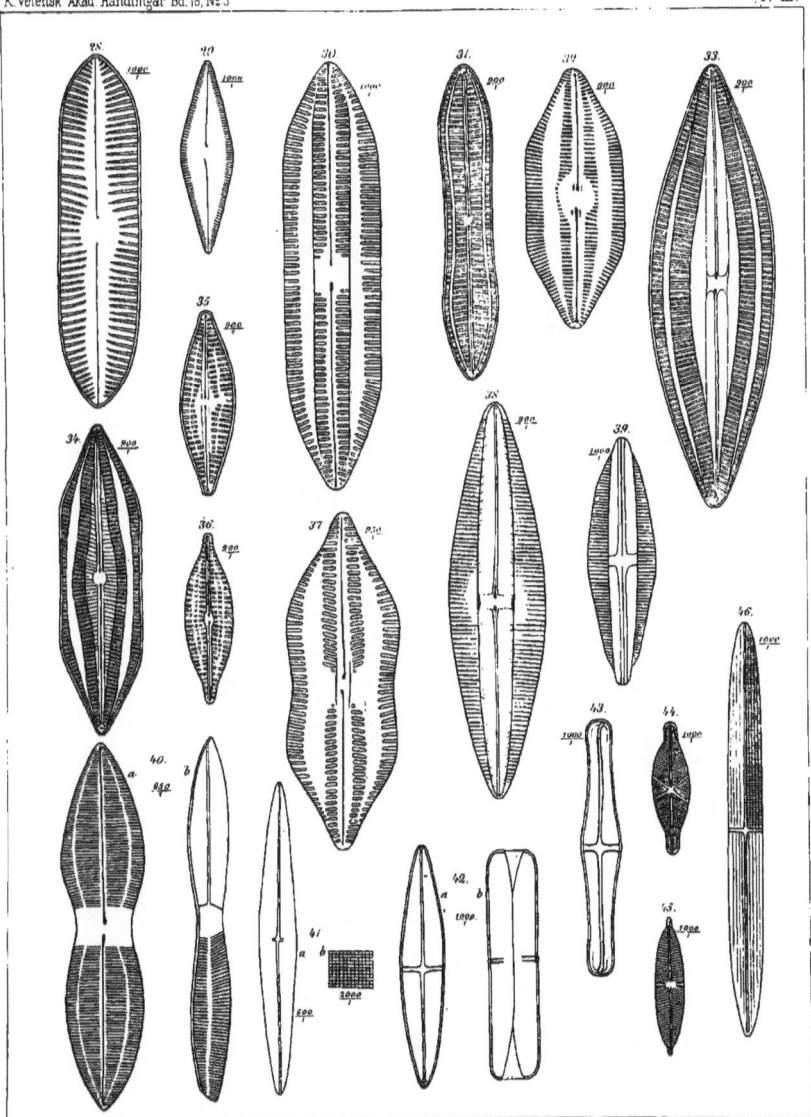

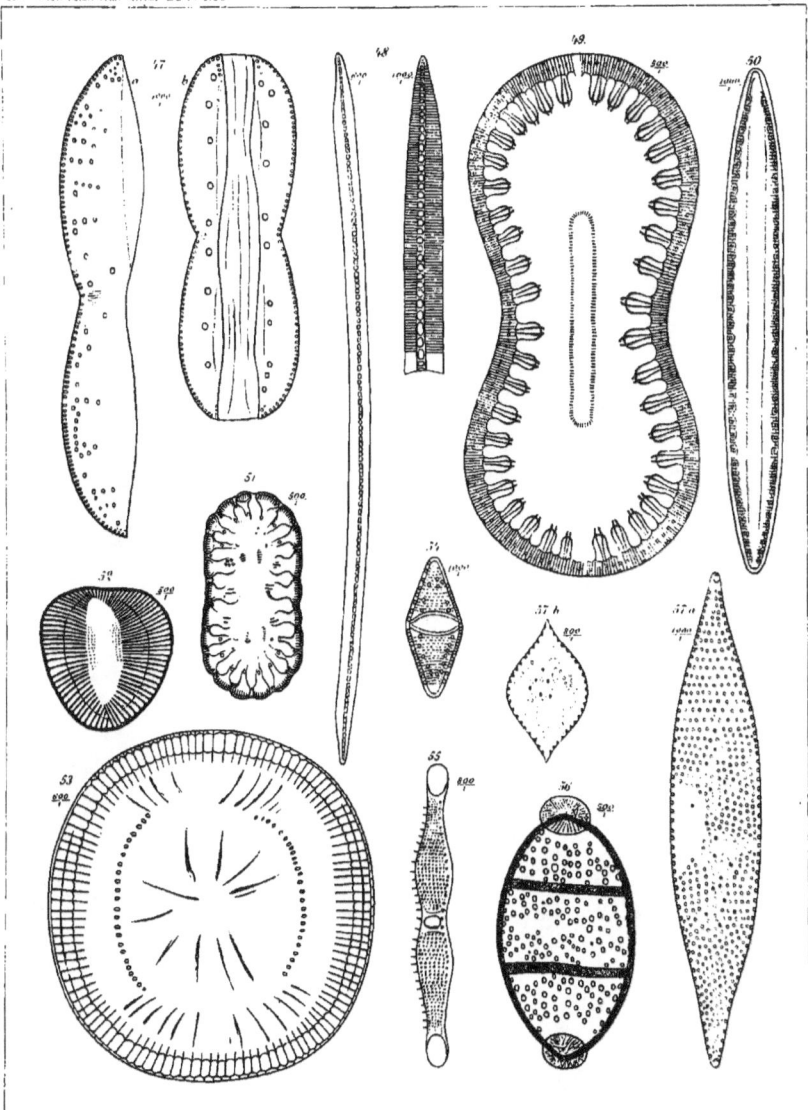

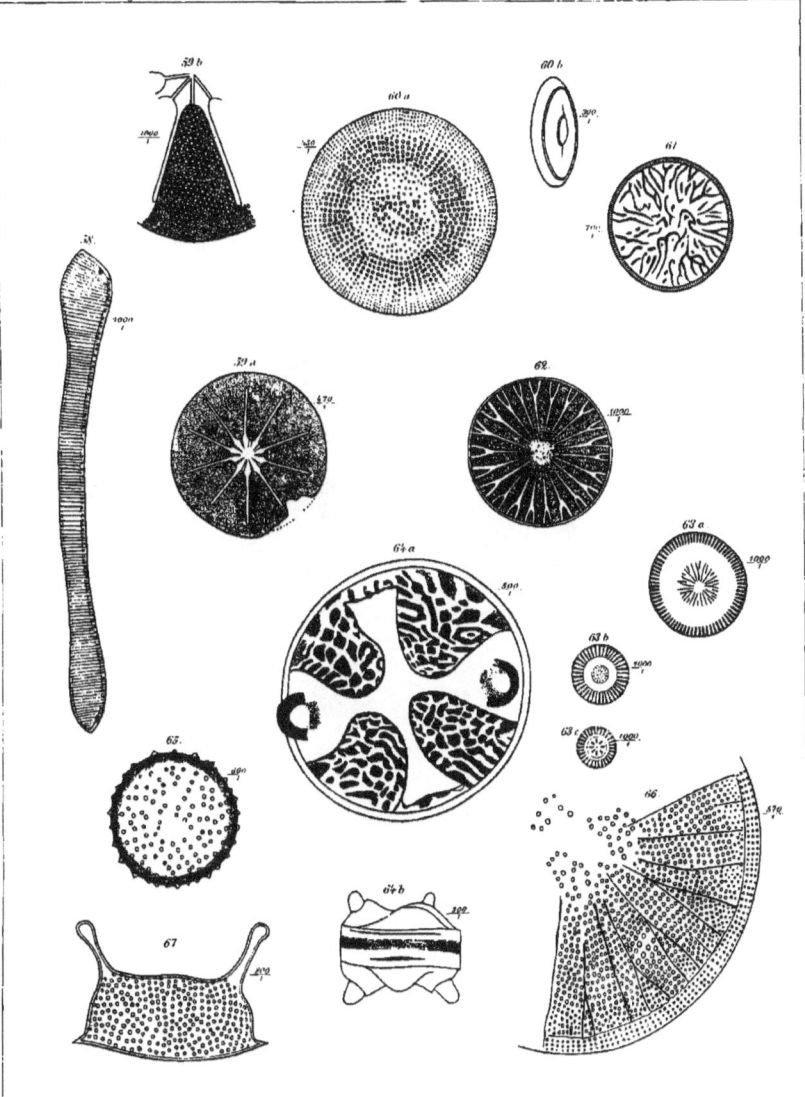

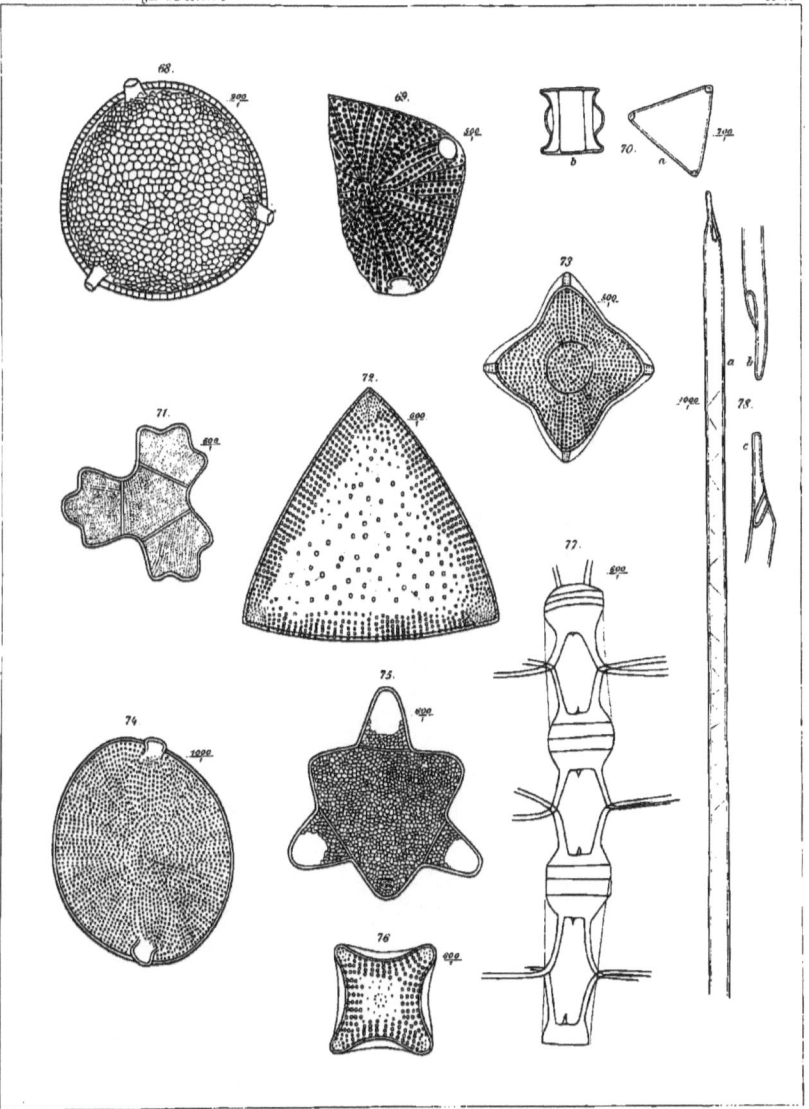

*with compliments
from
P T Cleve*

P. T. Cleve.
Plankton collected by the
Swedish Expedition to Spitzbergen
in 1898.

1899.

PLANKTON

COLLECTED BY

THE SWEDISH EXPEDITION TO SPITZBERGEN IN 1898

EXAMINED

BY

P. T. CLEVE

WITH 4 PLATES

PRESENTED TO THE R. SWEDISH ACADEMY OF SCIENCES 1899 MARCH 8TH

STOCKHOLM
KUNGL. BOKTRYCKERIET. P. A. NORSTEDT & SÖNER
1899

The scientific Swedish expedition 1898 to Spitzbergen under the direction of Professor A. G. NATHORST paid a particular interest in exploring the plankton of the sea. A great number of samples were gathered, among which about 50 were collected by pumping the water through a silk-net. These gatherings were all small and have been completely examined by me both for animal and vegetable plankton. The other samples, about 100, were brought up by the tow-net, partly from the surface and partly from more or less considerable depths. As Dr. C. AURIVILLIUS has charged himself with the examination of the animals in all the tow-net gatherings, I have examined them for vegetable plankton only, with the exception of the radiolarians, which offered a particular interest for my other plankton-researches.

Plankton-types.

I proposed in 1896[1] to class the plankton of the Atlantic and its tributaries in certain types or formations according to the association of species. For understanding the following it will be necessary first to characterize briefly these plankton-types.

I. **Desmo-plankton** (sign D). This formation rules in the warmest part of the Atlantic, in the Sargasso-sea and in the equatorial current.

The *temperature* of the water containing desmo-plankton varies usually between 20° and 28° and the *salinity* is about 36 p. m.

The organisms belong to a great number of species, many of which are identical with those of the Indian Ocean. Among the more characteristic species I can name the following:

Animals.	Plants.
Clausocalanus furcatus,	*Trichodesmium*,
Corycæus longicaudis,	*Pyrocystis pseudonoctiluca*,
C. speciosus,	*Ceratium fusus* var. *longiseta* (n. v.),
Euchæta marina,	*C. tripos* var. *flagellifera* (n. v.),
Miracia efferata,	*Ceratocorys horrida*,
Oncæa venusta,	*Goniodoma acuminatum*,
Setella gracilis,	*Ornithocercus magnificus*,
Radiolarians (many species).	*Chætoceros coarctatus*,
	C. tetrastichon,
	Climacodium biconcavum,
	C. Frauenfeldii (= *C. Jacobi* CL.),
	Hemiaulus Hauckii.

[1] Bih. till K. Sv. Vet.-Akad. Handl. XXII, 3, N:o 5. — A treatise on the phyto-plankton. Upsala 1897.

II. **Styliplankton** (Sign *S*). The region of desmoplankton, which is subject to variation in extent according to the seasons, is surrounded by an irregular band of water containing styliplankton. In the west this plankton-type seems always to occur in mixture with desmoplankton, and such a mixture characterizes the Caribbean Sea, the Antilles-current to the region of Bermuda. About the 40° breadth the styliplankton becomes more differentiated and the region increases in breadth towards the European and African coasts. It forms a narrow band west of Africa from Cape Verde to Canaries and occupies the triangular space between the Azores, the English Channel and Bermuda. The extent of the region is subject to great variation according to the seasons. In the summer it approaches towards the Fårōe Channel (probably also towards Iceland) in a mighty tongue, which sends branches through the English Channel into the German Ocean and around Scotland into the North Sea. When the water enters the North Sea its salinity becomes lowered by admixture of the continental coast-water and, consequently, the plankton becomes also modified. Some of the species die away, others multiply, and thus are originated in the North Sea two important *derived styli-planktontypes, the tripos-plankton in the north and the didymus-plankton in the south*. I have distinguished as a third type of North Sea plankton the *halosphæra-plankton*. This kind also originates from the styliplankton by an considerable increase of the green alga Halosphæra viridis, which seems to take place in the autumn around Fårōe, from whence it descends to Scotland and enters the North Sea finally reaching Skagerack.

The styliplankton-water, which in the beginning of the summer reaches the Fårōe Channel proceeds during the autumn towards Spitzbergen.

The *temperature* of this water varies usually between 10° and 20° and the *salinity* is about 35 p. m.

The number of *organisms* constituting the styliplankton is very considerable and the flora and fauna are subject to a great variability according to the breadth and the season. Some species appear simultaneously at the African and South American coasts, others occur in the whole region, others again seem to be limited to the eastern part. I name among the more common and characteristic forms the following, marking with *e* such forms, as occur in the eastern Atlantic. With *s* I denote forms, which as a rule do not pass over the Fårōe Channel, and with *n* forms which enter the northern Atlantic.

Animals.

Acartia Clausii (*e n*),
Centropages typicus (*n*),
Clausocalanus arcuicornis (*s*),
Corycæus rostratus (*e s*),
Mecynocera Clausi (in the spring *s*),
Microsetella atlantica (*n*),
Oithona plumifera (*s, n* rarely),
O. similis (*n*),
Oncæa minuta (*e n*),
Paracalanus parvus (*n*),

Plants.

Halosphæra viridis (*n*),
Ceratium (trip. v.) *auritum* (*e s*),
C. candelabrum (*s*),
C. furca (*e n*),
C. lineatum (*n*),
C. reticulatum (*s*),
Dinophysis homunculus (*s*),
Diplopsalis lenticula (*n*),
Gonyaulax polygramma (*n*),
Peridinium divergens (*n*),

Temora stylifera (s),
Sagitta bipunctata (n),
Globigerina bulloides (n),
Codonella lagenula (s),
Cyttarocylis acuminata (s),
C. cassis (s),
C. ganymedes (s),
C. Treforti (s),
Dictyocysta elegans (e n),
D. mitra (s),
Tintinnus Fraknoi (s).

Peridinium oblongum[1] (n),
Chætoceros furca (s),
C. Lorenziana (s),
C. volans (n),
Corethron hystrix (e n),
Coscinodiscus sol (e),
Dactyliosolen antarcticus (e n),
Hemidiscus cuneiformis,
Rhizosolenia alata (n),
R. gracillima (n),
R. styliformis (n).

The derived stylitypes of the North Sea, the *didymus-* and *tripos-plankton*, are characterized as follows.

A. **Didymus-plankton** (Sign *Nm*). This plankton-type rules in the summer and autumn along the southern coasts of the German Ocean above the 50 metre-plateau of the bottom.

The *temperature* varies between 8° and 17° and the salinity is about 32 or 33 p. m.

The organisms are numerous and the diatoms constitute an important part of them. Among the animals many are common to didymus- and triposplankton and their names are in the following lists enclosed in parenthesis. As the more common species we note:

Animals.

(*Acartia Clausii*),
(*Centropages hamatus*),
(*C. typicus*),
Corycæus anglicus,
Isias clavipes,
Labidocera Wollastonii,
(*Oithona similis*),
(*Paracalanus parvus*),
Podon polyphemoides,
(*Sagitta bipunctata*),
Oikopleura dioica,
Noctiluca miliaris,
Tintinnopsis campanula.

Plants.

Bacteriastrum varians,
Biddulphia mobilensis,
Cerataulina Bergonii,
Chætoceros curvisetus,
C. danicus,
C. didymus,
C. Schüttii,
C. Weissflogii,
Ditylum Brightwellii,
Eucampia zodiacus,
Guinardia flaccida,
Rhizosolenia Shrubsolii,
R. Stolterfothii,
Streptotheca tamesis.

B. **Triposplankton** (Sign *Tp*) rules in the summer and autumn in the northern part of the North Sea above the 100 metre-plateau of the bottom and extends from Scotland to Scandinavia as far as Finmarken. In the spring it is replaced by water with chæto-plankton.

---

[1] *Perid. divergens v. oblonga* AURIV.

The *temperature* varies usually between about 5° in the winter and 14° in the summer, and the salinity is about 34 p. m., but these figures are subject to great variations according to relative abundance of oceanic or coast-water that enters in the composition of the triposplankton-water.

The triposplankton is chiefly constituted by cilioflagellates and entomostraca, the diatoms being almost absent. As stated above the animals are to a great extent of the same species as in the didymusplankton, which is easily explained as both types are derived from styliplankton.

Among the organisms we note the following:

Animals.
(*Sagitta bipunctata*),
(*Acartia Clausii*),
Anomalocera Patersonii,
Calanus finmarchicus,
(*Centropages typicus*),
(*Oithona similis*),
(*Paracalanus parvus*),
Pseudocalanus elongatus,
Temora longicornis,
Evadne Nordmannii,
E. spinifera,
Podon intermedius.

Plants.
Ceratium furca,
C. fusus,
C. tripos,
C. trip. v. macroceros,
Peridinium divergens.

Many of the species of the styliplankton also enter into the triposplankton, as *Acanthometron quadrifolium*. *Plectophora arachnoides*, probably originally belonging to the chætoplankton and abundant around Scotland, enters also frequently into the triposplankton.

III. **Chætoplankton** (Sign *C*). This planktontype occurs in the western and northern parts of the Atlantic only and during the spring. From March to June or July it can be traced from about the 40° Lat. and 70° Long. to the Newfoundland Banks and to the south of Iceland, from whence it turns across the Färöe Channel and enters the North Sea, replacing its triposplankton, and reaches the coasts of Scandinavia. It disappears in the summer, becoming replaced by styliplankton, but rules in July and August around Spitzbergen. When the water with the chætoplankton touches the coasts, especially of Iceland, it sweeps away the neritic plankton there and spreads it along the coasts of Scotland and Scandinavia, where it enters into the fjords. Thus many species of northern origin may remain during the summer emprisoned in the fjords, especially in their deeper water.

The *temperature* of the chætoplankton-water varies usually between 5° and 9° and the *salinity* is about 35 p. m.

The organisms of the chætoplankton are chiefly diatoms, especially *Chætoceros decipiens* and *Ch. constrictus*. *C. borealis* and *C. criophilus* occur both in chæto- and trichoplankton so that it is difficult to decide whether they belong to one or the other type.

Another organism, the flagellate *Phæocystis Pouchetii*, appears in the same time as Chætoceros decipiens, frequently in great abundance, and has about the same distribution. I therefore include also that organism among the chæto-species.

IV. **Trichoplankton** (Sign *T*). This type rules in the western Atlantic and constitutes in the summer the plankton of the Irminger Sea. Its origin is doubtful. Typical trichoplankton was gathered in the Bering Sea during the expedition of the Vega and it is an open question whether it spreads from the northern Pacific to the northern Atlantic or vice versa. In the winter (1897—98) the characteristic species of the trichoplankton appeared as far down to the south as to the south of the Azores, which possibly may be owing to the plankton of the Labrador-current having been conveyed by the south-going branch of the Gulf-stream. In the summer it is confined to the western and arctic Atlantic, but in the winter it spreads to Scandinavia. The *temperature* of the trichoplankton-water varies between 6° and 12° and the salinity amounts to about 34 p. m.

As the trichoplankton frequently becomes mixed with chætoplankton and with siraplankton it is a difficult matter to make out to what type a number of species really belong. I consider the following as chiefly tricho-organisms:

Animals.

Calanus finmarchicus,
Fritillaria borealis,
Spadella hamata,
Cyttarocylis denticulata (with the varieties *edentula, media* and *gigantea*),
Ptychocylis acuta,
Tintinnus minutus.

Plants.

Ceratium tripos v. arctica,
Chætoceros atlanticus,
Coscinodiscus oculus iridis,
Rhizosolenia obtusa,
R. semispina,
Thalassiosira gravida,
Thalassiothrix longissima.

On the coasts, washed by the trichoplankton-water, there originates a peculiar kind of derived trichoplankton, which I have designated as

Northern neritic plankton (Sign *Ns*). This somewhat variable type occurs at the coast of Iceland, in Skagerack and in the fjords of Sweden during the winter, also in the fjords of Norway and on the Norwegian coast-banks, where it becomes in the summer slowly replaced by triposplankton. This kind of plankton seems to invade the coasts of Scotland and Scandinavia twice a year, viz. in the spring in company or in connection with the chætoplankton and in the autumn in connection with the trichoplankton. The detailed study of this kind of plankton will doubtless afford very interesting results as different species rule on different coasts. Thus for instance the *Asterionella spathulifera* abounds in the south coast of Iceland and becomes from thence transported to Scotland and as far southwards as to the coast of Holland. On the coast-banks of Norway *Ceratium tripos v. longipes* is the ruling species. The Limfjord of Denmark affords particular advantages for the development of some species, as *Skeletonema costatum* and *Chætoceros debilis*,[1] which remain there for the greater part of the year.

---

[1] C. G. T. PETERSEN. Beretning fra den danske biologiske Station 1898.

The *temperature* of the water with northern neritic plankton varies in Skagerak from about 4° to 7° and the *salinity* is about 32—33 p. m.

As species constituting the northern neritic plankton we name the following:

Animals.	Plants.
(*Acartia longiremis*),	*Asterionella spathulifera*,
(*Calanus finmarchicus*),	*Biddulphia aurita*,
(*Centropages hamatus*),	*Chætoceros debilis*,
(*Pseudocalanus elongatus*),	*C. diadema*,
(*Temora longicornis*),	*C. scolopendra*,
Tintinnopsis beroidea,	*C. teres*,
T. ventricosa.	*Coscinodiscus polychordus*,
	Leptocylindrus danicus,
	Skeletonema costatum,
	Thalassiosira gelatinosa,
	Thalassiothrix Frauenfeldii,
	Ceratium tripos v. longipes,
	Gonyaulax spinifera,
	Peridinium depressum.

V. **Sira-plankton** (Sign *Si*) rules along the coasts of Greenland and in Baffins Bay, or in the Arctic Ocean properly, where it constitutes the plankton of the water with melting drift-ice. As it touches the trichoplankton it becomes frequently mixed with it, so that the distinction of what species belong to one or the other is a matter of difficulty. The water with sira-plankton has lower temperature than the trichoplankton-water and less salinity, about 32—33. This type might be considered as a kind of neritic plankton, did not the most characteristic species, *Thalassiosira Nordenskiöldii*, at certain periods occur in wide areas north of the Kara Sea and between Spitzbergen and Finmarken. Typical sira-plankton is almost free from animals and contains as its most characteristic species *Thalassiosira Nordenskiöldii*, *Fragilaria oceanica*, *Lauderia fragilis*, *Chætoceros furcellatus* and *C. socialis*. It is frequently mixed with some northern neritic forms as *Chætoceros debilis*, *C. diadema*, *C. scolopendra*, *Coscinodiscus oculus iridis*, *Biddulphia aurita*, *Thalassiosira gravida* etc.

This kind of plankton appears in Skagerak usually in February and March.

Along the coast of Greenland the sira-plankton becomes mixed with a number of neritic forms and such a derived sira-plankton I have distinguished as

Arctic neritic plankton (sign *Ng*). This kind of plankton contains, besides the species of sira-plankton, the following:

Amphiprora hyperborea,	*Eucampia groenlandica*,
Achnanthes tæniata,	*Fragilaria cylindrus*,
Chætoceros septentrionalis,	*Navicula septentrionalis*,
Coscinodiscus bioculatus,	*Nitzschia frigida*,
C. hyalinus,	*Pleurosigma Stuxbergii*.

Surface-plankton.

In the following account of the plankton, gathered by the Swedish expedition to Spitzbergen in 1898, I distinguish, as usually, with *c* common, *cc* very common, *ccc* the principal mass, with + neither common nor rare, with *r* rare, and *rr* some few specimens only. In case of scarcity of the plankton I enclose the sign by one or two parentheses and where no plankton was found I use 0.

1. Lindesnäs—Lofoten.

May 27th to June 1th.

Temperature varying between 7° and 9°. Salinity 33—35 p. m.

The plankton is of great uniformity, being a mixture of tripos- and northern neritic plankton (*Tp, Ns*).

The most important species are the following:

Of triposplankton:
Acartia Clausii +,
Microsetella atlantica r,
Oithona similis +,
Evadne Nordmannii c,
E. spinifera c,
Podon intermedius r,
Halosphæra viridis r,
Ceratium furca +,
C. fusus +,
C. tripos r,
C. trip. v. macroceros c,
Rhizosolenia styliformis rr.

Of northern neritic plankton:
Acartia longiremis c,
Ceratium tripos var. *longipes* cc,
Peridinium depressum +,
Coscinodiscus oculus iridis rr.

Common to both:
Calanus finmarchicus +,
Temora longicornis +.

One sample only (63° 13′ N 5° 15′ E.) contained *Leptocylindrus danicus* in abundance.

The plankton of this region agrees completely with that of June 1896.[1] If compared with the plankton of May 1897 in the same region, we mark that the triposplankton occurred in 1898 in greater abundance. This corresponds with the lower temperature (5,45—9,72) and salinity (28,05 to 34,11) in the year 1897.

---
[1] Bih. till K. Sv. Vet.-Akad. Handl. XXIII, 2, N:o 4.

2. Lofoten—Beeren Eiland.

June 2d to June 12th.

Temperature 7,55 to 5,15; near Beeren Eiland 2,40. Salinity 34—35.

The ruling plankton is chætoplankton, mixed with variable amounts of tricho- and styliplankton.

In the chætoplankton:	In the trichoplankton:	In the styliplankton:
Plectophora arachnoides r,	*Calanus finmarchicus* c,	*Oithona plumifera* rr,
Chætoceros criophilus c,	*Chætoceros criophilus* c,	*Collozoum inerme* +,
C. decipiens c,	*Coscinodiscus oculus iridis* r,	*Chætoceros volans* +.
Phæocystis Pouchetii (c near	*Rhizosolenia semispina* +,	
Beeren Eiland).	*Thalassiothrix longissima* r.	

Interesting is the occurrence of the styliplanktonforms, of which *Oithona plumifera* and *Collozoum* indicate a far distant origin (probably the region of the Azores). *Plectophora arachnoides* indicates that the water has passed the Faröe Channel.

In June 1896 and May 1897 this region was almost sterile, containing traces only of northern neritic plankton.

3. Beeren Eiland—Hope Island.

June 20th to June 23d.

Temperature —0,35 to +0,97 and salinity 34,76 to 32,97.

The ruling plankton is chætoplankton with *Chætoceros decipiens* and *Phæocystis Pouchetii;* tricho-plankton is also represented by *Calanus finmarchicus, Cyttarocylis gigantea* and *Coscinodiscus oculus iridis,* and arctic neritic plankton by the rare occurrence of *Ptychocylis obtusa.*

4. Hope Island—Icefjord.

June 24th.

Temperature 0,8 to 3,0. Salinity 33,80 to 35,06.

An almost sterile region with some few specimens of *Phæocystis Pouchetii* (C) and *Thalassiosira Nordenskiöldii, Chætoceros furcellatus, Ptychocylis obtusa* and *Peridinium pellucidum* (*Ng*).

5. Icefjord—Swedish Depth—Süd Cape.

July 26th to August 2d.

The plankton is subject to great variation, occurs as a rule sparingly and belongs to chæto-, styli- and tricho-plankton. In August 1896 chæto-plankton chiefly ruled in this region.

Month	VII	VII	VII	VII	VIII
Day	26	26	30	31	1
Lat.	76° 13′	77° 53′	76° 12′	77° 14′	76° 36′
Long.	7° 30′ E.	5° 3′ E.	0° 17′ W.	6° 34′ E.	12° 8′ E.
Temp.	5,34	4,76	4,59	5,85	7,38
Sal.	34,89	34,57	34,58	34,77	35,12
Pl.-type	(*Ng S*)	(*T C*)	(*T C*)	*T S*	*T S*
Calanus finmarchicus	.	.	.	r	.
Oithona similis	r	.	+	.	!·
Euthemisto libellula	r	.	.	.	.
Cyttarocylis edentulata	.	r	c	cc	.
C. media	r	r	+	.	.
Ptychocylis obtusa	r	.	.	.	.
Litholophus ligurinus	r	.	.	.	.
Ceratium (trip. v.) arcticum	r	r	r	.	+
C. (trip. v.) longipes	.	.	.	.	r
Peridinium pellucidum	r	+	c	.	.
Chætoceros borealis	.	r	.	.	r
C. decipiens	.	+	c	.	.
C. volans	.	.	.	c	+
Rhizosolenia gracillima	.	.	.	c	.
R. obtusa	.	r	.	.	.
R. semispina	.	.	.	.	c

6. Süd Cape—King Charles Land.

August 3d to August 6th.

Much drift-ice. Temperature 1 to 3,94. Salinity 30,98 to 34,45.

The plankton consists chiefly of *chætoplankton*, mixed with *trichoplankton* and a little arctic neritic plankton. *Oithona similis* was also found.

The more important species were the following:

Chætopl..

Chætoceros decipiens +,
Phæocystis Pouchetii r.

Trichopl.:

Calanus finmarchicus r,
Cyttarocylis denticulata r,
    var. obtusa r,
    var. gigantea c,
    var. media r,
Tintinnus minutus r,
Ceratium (trip v.) arcticum c,
Coscinodiscus oculus iridis +,
Rhizosolenia semispina r.

Arctic neritic pl.:

Peridinium pellucidum +,
Ptychocylis obtusa +.

7. King Charles Land. Round Spitzbergen. North west of Spitzbergen.
August 13th. August 25th.

Temperature —0,58 to +3,44. Salinity about 33 p. m.
The plankton is constituted by chæto-, tricho- and arctic neritic plankton.
The following were the most important:

Chætopl.	Trichopl.	Arctic neritic plankton.
Chætoceros borealis +,	*Calanus finmarchicus* r,	*Cyttarocylis dentic. v. obtusa* c,
C. criophilus r,	*Fritillaria borealis* r,	*Fungella arctica* r,
C. decipiens +,	*Cyttarocylis denticulata* r,	*Ptychocylis obtusa* c,
Phæocystis Pouchetii r.	v. *gigantea* c,	*Dinobryum* c,
	v. *media* r,	*Peridinium pellucidum* +.
	Tintinnus borealis r,	
	Ceratium arcticum c,	
	Chætoceros atlanticus r,	
	C. boreal. v. Brightwellii r,	
	C. criophilus r,	
	Coscinodiscus oculus iridis rr,	
	Rhizosolenia obtusa r,	
	Thalassiosira gravida r.	

Besides these species were found *Oithona similis*, common in some gatherings, and the following of the northern neritic plankton: *Ceratium (tripos v.) longipes* r, *Chætoceros diadema* r, *Leptocylindrus danicus* r.

8. West of Spitzbergen—Beeren Eiland.
August 28th to September 4th.

Temperature 5,34 to 7,24. Salinity about 35.
The plankton is composed of styliplankton, usually predominant, and trichoplankton. The most important forms are:

Styliplankton.	Trichoplankton.
Microsetella atlantica r,	*Calanus finmarchicus*,
Oithona similis c,	*Fritillaria borealis*,
Oncæa minuta +,	*Cyttarocylis denticulata* r,
Globigerina bulloides r.	var. *media* c,
Challengeria tridens r,	var. *edentula* +,
Litholophus ligurinus r.	var. *gigantea* r,
Chætoceros borealis v. solitaria +,	*Ptychocylis acuta* r,
C. volans cc,	*Tintinnus secatus* r,
Corethron hystrix r,	*T. minutus* r,
Rhizosolenia alata r,	*Ceratium tripos v. arctica* r,

R. *gracillima* (in some spots),   *Chætoceros atlanticus* r,
R. *hebetata* +,   *C. criophilus* +,
R. *styliformis* r to c.   *Rhizosolenia obtusa* r to c,
                                  Thalassiosira gravida r,
                                  Thalassiothrix longissima rr.

Among these species some are of a particular interest, for instance *Challengeria tridens* and *Plectophora arachnoides*, radiolarians known from the Färöe Channel. *Litholophus ligurinus* and the still more interesting *Oncæa minuta* can be traced from the Mediterranean and the Azores to the mouth of the English Channel and Färöe Channel, thus indicating the course the styliplankton-water has taken.

In the year 1896 in August this region west of Spitzbergen was sterile, and north of Beeren Eiland there ruled typical trichoplankton. I July 1897 chætoplankton was preponderant west of Spitzbergen and was north of Beeren Eiland mixed with trichoplankton. Styliplankton appeared very sparingly at first south of Beeren Eiland.

9. Beeren Eiland—Fuglö.
September 4th to September 6th.

Temperature 8,8 to 9,4c. Salinity about 35.

The plankton is constituted, as north of Beeren Eiland, of *styli-* and *tricho*plankton, but with an admixture of triposplankton and northern (Norwegian) neritic plankton.

Styli- and tripos-plankton.

Acartia Clausii r to +,
Microsetella atlantica r,
Oithona similis + to cc,
Oncæa minuta r,
Acanthometron quadrifolium c,
Acanthonia Mülleri r,
(*Plectophora arachnoides* r),
Globigerina bulloides r,
Halosphæra viridis c,
Ceratium furca r to c,
C. fusus r to +,
C. tripos +,
C. trip. v. macroceros cc,
Peridinium divergens +,
Corethron hystrix r,
Rhizosolenia alata r,
R. gracillima r to +,
R. hebetata r.

Tricho- and northern neritic plankton.

Calanus finmarchicus c,
Cyttarocylis denticulata r,
   v. *gigantea* c,
   v. *media* r,
Ptychocylis acuta r,
Ceratium tripos v. longipes c,
Peridinium depressum r.

It follows from the above analysis of the plankton-gatherings that in the year 1898 the styliplankton was by far more richly represented than in the two precedent years.

Deep-sea Plankton.

At some stations plankton was gathered by hauls from different depths. As Dr. AURIVILLIUS will describe the animals found in these samples, I have examined the vegetable plankton and the radiolarians only, and being thus unable to give a complete account of these gatherings I confine myself here to shortly characterizing them so far as regards the phytoplankton and the radiolarians.

1. **Station M.** 26 to 27 July. Lat. 77° 39'. Long. 1° 18' E. 100—0 metres. Salinity at 100 m. 34,97, in the surface 32,22. Temp. 5,07.

This sample contained trichoplankton (*Chætoceros criophilus, Rhizosolenia obtusa*) and some arctic neritic plankton (*Dinobryum*), but the animals indicate the presence of an amount of styliplankton of the same kind as in the surface west and south of Spitzbergen in August and September.

2. **Station N.** 28 July. Lat. 77° 52' N. Long. 3° 5' W.
   a. *Haul 10—0 m.* Temp. at 0 m. 3,63. Salinity 34,38. Chiefly chætoplankton (*Chætoceros decipiens, Phæocystis Pouchetii*) and arctic neritic plankton (*Dinobryum*).
   b. *Haul 25—0 m.* Temp. at 25 m. 2,72. Salinity 34,74. The same kind of plankton.
   c. *Haul 100—0 m.* Sal. at 100 m. 35,03. Plankton sparingly (*Phæocystis Pouchetii*).
   d. *Haul 500—0 m.* Temp. at 100 m. +0,83. Sal. 35,03. Content the same as a, but, in addition, *Rhizosolenia gracillima* and some animals of the styliplankton-type.

The conclusion is, that the deeper strata contained styliplankton, the upper chætoplankton.

3. **Station O.** 29 to 30 July. Lat. 78° 13' N. Long. 2° 58' W.
   a. *Haul 100—0 m.* Temp. at 0 m. 3,1, sal. 33,76; at 100 m. 1,17, sal. 35,03. Content: chiefly *Phæocystis Pouchetii*, thus chætoplankton.
   b. *Haul 500—0 m.* Temp. at 500 m. 0,95, sal. 35,03. Content as a, and besides, rarely *Challengeria tridens* and some other styliplankton forms.
   c. *Haul 2,600—0 m.* Temp. at 2,700 m. —1,48, sal. 34,96. Chiefly as a but with radiolarians of many species sparingly. Among the radiolarians were found a number of new forms which will be described further on. Among known forms *Aulacantha lævissima, Challengeria tridens* and *Trochodiscus echinidiscus* are known from the Faröe Channel, *Stichopilium Davisianum* from the bottom mud near Greenland, also *Artrostrobus annulatus*, which latter was first found near Kamtchatka. *Dictyophimus gracilipes* is known from Kamtchatka only. *Challengeria Harstoni* was dredged by the Challenger-expedition from the abysmal depths east of Japan. Among the new forms is *Polypetta holostoma*, allied to *P. tabulata* from the central Indian Ocean. *Aulodendron antarcticum, Auloscena spectabilis* and *Sagenoscena penicillata* are known from the Antarctic Ocean only.

4. **Station P.** August 1th. Lat. 76° 36' N. Long. 12° 13' E.
a. *Haul 25—0 m.* Temp. at 0 m. 7,1, at 25 m. 5,8. Sal. at 0 m. and at 25 m. 35,12. Styliplankton and trichoplankton as west of Spitzbergen.
b. *Haul 50—0 m.* Temp. at 50 m. 4,98. Sal. 35,13. Similar to a.
c. *Haul 100—0 m.* Temp. at 100 m. 3,75. Sal. 35,05. Similar to a.
d. *Haul 500—0 m.* Temp. at 500 m. 2,5. Sal. 35,10. As a, but contained some radiolarians, as *Artrotrobus annulatus*, *Dictyophimus gracilipes*, *Acanthocorys umbellifera*.

5. **Station S.** Aug. 20th. Lat. 81° 14'. Long. 22° 50' E.
a. *Haul 10—0 m.* Temp. at 0 m. 0,38, sal. 32,49. Temp. at 10 m. 1,18, sal. 33,42. Plankton chiefly trichoplankton (most common: *Chætoceros borealis*, *C. bor. v. Brightwelli*, *C. criophilus*, *Rhizosolenia obtusa* and *Thalossiosira gravida*) and sparingly arctic neritic plankton (*Chætoceros diadema*, *Leptocylindrus danicus*).
b. *Haul 25—0 m.* Temp. at 30 m. 3,3. Sal. 34,41. The same as a.
c. *Haul 130—0 m.* Temp. at 100 m. 1,7, at 150 m. 1,98. Sal. at 100 m. 34,77, at 150 m. 34,83. Plankton as in a, but some animals indicate the presence of styliplankton.

6. **Station T.** August 27th. Lat. 79° 58' N. Long. 9° 35' E.
a. *Haul 10—0 m.* Temp. at 0 m. 4,58. S. 34,53. This gathering contained the following:

Chætoplankton.	Trichoplankton with northern and arctic neritic plankton.	Styliplankton.
Chætoceros borealis r,	*Chætoceros atlanticus* r,	*Rhizosolenia gracillima* +,
C. criophilus c,	*C. borealis* r,	*R. hebetata* r,
C. decipiens r,	var. *Brightwellii* +,	*R. styliformis* r.
Phæocystis Pouchetii +.	*C. criophilus* c,	
	C. diadema c,	
	C. teres r,	
	Leptocylindrus danicus r,	
	Thalassiosira gravida c,	
	Dinobryum r.	

The plankton is thus constituted principally of trichoplankton with some arctic or northern neritic plankton and contains a small amount of chæto- and styliplankton.
b. *Haul 100—0 m.* Temp. at 100 m. 3,7. Sal. 35,12. Plankton similar to a, but contained besides *Globigerina*, *Challengeria tridens*, *Plectophora arachnoides*, which indicate an increased amount of styliplankton.
c. *Haul 400—0 m.* Temp. at 430 m. 1,5. Sal. 35,06.
Similar to b but with some additional styliplankton-forms as *Diplopsalis lenticula* (rr), *Chæt. borealis var. solitaria* (r), *Chætos. volans* (r), *Oithona plumifera*, *Oncæa minuta*, indicating an increased amount of styliplankton. This sample was examined for radiolarians, of which several new forms were found. Among known species were found *Challengeria Harstoni* and *Dictyophimus gracilipes* as in the deep-sea haul at the station O

and besides *Acanthocorys umbellifera* (stylipl.) and *Theocalyptra cornuta*, the last named being known from Kamtchatka and Greenland and found by me this year (7. III) in the surface at 63° 1' N. and 1° 36' E.

The conclusion is that the water below 100 m. contains styliplankton and is covered with a sheet of trichoplankton-water.

7. **Station U.** September 1th. Lat. 75° 50'. Long. 15° 25' E.

a. *Haul 2—0 m.* Temp. at 0 m. 5,73. Sal. 34,91. The plankton contained:

Chætoplankton.	Tricho- and northern neritic plankton.	Styliplankton.
Chætoceros criophilus cc,	*Chætoceros criophilus* cc,	*Rhizosolenia styliformis* r.
C. decipiens rr.	*C. diadema* c,	
	C. laciniosus r.	

Chiefly trichopl. with traces only of styli- and chætopl.

b. *Haul 100—0 m.* Similar to a.

c. *Haul 320—0 m.* Temp. at 350 m. 2,73. Sal. 35,13. Similar to a, but also with animals of the stylitype (*Oithona plumifera, Oncæa minuta, Challengeria tridens* etc.). This sample was examined for radiolarians, of which were found *Challengeria Harstoni, Acanthocorys umbellifera, Theocalyptra cornuta, Dictyophimus gracilipes* etc. indicating the same kind of water as in the deeper strata at St. O, T etc.

8. **Station X.** September 5th. Lat. 71° 50'. Long. 19° 2' E.

a. *Haul 25—0 m.* Temp. at 0 m. 9,08. Sal. 34,96.

Northern neritic plankton.	Styli- and triposplankton.
Ceratium tripos v. longipes c,	*Halosphæra viridis* +,
Dinophysis acuta r,	*Ceratium furca* +,
Gonyaulax spinifera r,	*C. fusus* r,
Peridinium depressum r,	*C. lineatum* rr,
P. ovatum r,	*C. tripos* +,
P. pellucidum r,	*C. trip. v. macroceros* c,
Chætoceros borealis v. Brightwellii r,	*Rhizosolenia alata* r.
C. contortus r.	*R. gracillima* cc,
	R. hebetata rr,
	R. styliformis rr.

The plankton contained, besides, *Globigerina, Acanthometron quadrifolium* and other species of the stylitype. The constituent plankton was thus styliplankton mixed with some northern neritic plankton.

b. *Haul 230—0 m.* Temp. at 200 m. 5,5. Sal. 35,13.

The plankton was nearly the same as in a and was examined for radiolarians. Among known forms were noted *Challengeria tridens, Acanthocorys umbellifera, Lithomitra lineata* and *Cromyomma zonaster*, the last named known from Greenland (2,000 m.).

The general result of this examination of the deep-sea gatherings might be summarized as follows:

The deeper strata with the sal. 35 contain chiefly styliplankton (from the eastern temperate Atlantic and Färöe Channel). This water reaches the surface at St. X.

The upper strata with 32—34 sal. contain at the stations N and O *chætoplankton*, at the stations M, P, S, T, U *trichoplankton*. As the latter type has been found this spring ruling in the region east of Greenland and north of Iceland it may derive from that part of the Ocean.

Organisms, found in the plankton-gatherings of the »Antarctic» 1898.

In the following I give a list of all the organisms, found by me in the plankton-gathering, as well as the dates etc. for every form. By »Temp.» I denote the temperature of the water in centigrades, by »Sal.» the salinity pro mille, by »Fq.» the frequency, whether *rr*, very rare, *r* rare, + not rare, *c* common, *cc* very common, or *ccc* principal constituent of the plankton. The sign × denotes dead specimens. By »Pl.» I understand the ruling plankton-type viz.: *C* chætoplankton, *Ng* arctic neritic plankton, *Nm* southern neritic plankton, *Ns* northern neritic plankton, *S* styliplankton, *T* trichoplankton and *Tp* triposplankton.

Amphipoda.

Euthemisto libellula (MANDT).
Surface: 26. VII. 78° 13' N. 7° 30' E. Temp. 5,38. Sal. 34,39.

Cladocera.

Evadne Nordmannii LOVÉN.

Surface:

Date.	Lat. N.	Long.	Temp.	Sal.	Fq.	Pl.
27 V	57° 50'	6° E.	8,70	33,69	c	*Tp Ns*
28 V	58° 14'	4° 40' E.	8,8	31,83	+	*Ns Tp*
28 V	58° 41'	4° 34' E.	8,00	33,04	+	*Ns Tp*
29 V	60° 13'	4° 24' E.	8,55	33,92	+	*Ns Tp*
5 IX	71° 57'	19° E.	9,08	34,90	+	*Tp (Ns)*

E. spinifera P. F. MÜLL.

Surface:

Date.	Lat. N.	Long.	Temp.	Sal.	Fq.	Pl.
27 V	57° 50'	6° E.	8,70	33,69	+	Tp Ns
29 V	60° 13'	4° 24' E.	8,35	33,32	r	Ns Tp
30 V	63° 13'	5° 15' E.	8,17	34,53	c	Tp Ns
30 V	63° 52'	6° 5' E.	8	34,53	c	Tp Ns

Podon intermedius LILLJEB.
Surface: 27 V. Lat. N. 57°50'. Long. 6° E. Temp. 8,70. Sal. 33,69. Fq. +. Pl. *Tp Ns*.

P. Leuckarti G. O. SARS.

Surface:

Date.	Lat. N.	Long.	Temp.	Sal.	Fq.	Pl.
27 V	57° 50'	6° E.	8,70	33,69	r	Tp Ns
29 V	60° 13'	4° 24' E.	8,35	33,32	+	Ns Tp

Copepoda.

Acartia Clausii GIESBR.

Surface:

Date.	Lat. N.	Long.	Temp.	Sal.	Fq.	Pl.
27 V	57° 50'	6° E.	8,70	33,69	+	Tp Ns
28 V	58° 14'	4° 40' E.	8,80	31,93	+	Ns Tp
28 V	58° 41'	4° 34' E.	8,30	33,04	+	Ns Tp
30 V	63° 52'	6° 5' E.	8	34,53	+	Tp Ns
1 VI	66° 42'	10° 30' E.	8,53	34,69	r	T s
10 VI	71° 10'	21°31' E.	6,71	35,20	+	C s
5 IX	71° 57'	19° E.	9,08	34,96	+	Tp (Ns)
5 IX	71° 14'	19°38' E.	9,40	34,92	r	Tp Ns

A. longiremis (LILLJEB.).

Surface:

Date.	Lat. N.	Long.	Temp.	Sal.	Fq.	Pl.
27 V	57° 50'	6° E.	8,70	33,69	+	Tp Ns
28 V	58° 14'	4° 40' E.	8,6	31,83	+	Ns Tp
28 V	58° 41'	4° 34' E.	8,30	33,04	c	Ns Tp
29 V	60° 13'	4° 24' E.	8,35	33,32	c	Ns Tp
30 V	63° 52'	6° 5' E.	8	34,53	r	Tp Ns

Calanus finmarchicus (GUNN.).

Surface:

Date	Lat. N.	Long.	Temp.	Sal.	Fq.	Pl.	Date	Lat. N.	Long.	Temp.	Sal.	Fq.	Pl.
27 V	57° 50'	6° E.	6,70	33,69	+	Tp Ns	21 VI	76° 27'	25°55' E.	0,24	33,66	n	(C)
28 V	58° 14'	4° 40' E.	8,8	31,83	+	Ns Tp	23 VI	77° 16'	27° 10' E.	0,97	33,15	c	(C)
28 V	58° 41'	4° 34' E.	8,30	33,04	+	Ns Tp	25 VI	76° 34'	17° 24' E.	0,6	33,80	+	
29 V	60° 13'	4° 24' E.	8,35	33,32	+	Ns Tp	28 VIII	78° 23'	10° 23' E.	6,06	34,94	cc	T
31 V	65° 34'	8° 45' E.	6,88	35,00	c	Ns T	29 VIII	77° 23'	10° 53' E.	5,55	35,08	r	T S
31 V	65° 47'	9° 10' E.	9,01	34,67	+	Ns Tp	2 IX	75° 24'	16° 47' E.	5,64	35,12	+	T (S)
1 VI	66° 42'	10° 30' E.	8,58	34,69	c	T Tp Ns	3 IX	74° 16'	18° 10' E.	2,88	34,86	ccc	T
2 VI	69° 15'	15° 25' E.	7,85	34,28	ccc	T	4 IX	72° 43'	18° 43' E.	8,8	35,01	c	Tp Ns
10 VI	71° 42'	22° 35' E.	6,40	35,15	cc	T C S	4 IX	72° 29'	18° 48' E.	8,87	35,04	c	Tp Ns
12 VI	73° 40'	22° 40' E.	2,40	35,05	c	C	5 IX	71° 14'	19° 38' E.	9,40	34,92	+	Tp Ns

Microsetella atlantica (BRADY & ROB.).

Surface:

Date	Lat. N.	Long.	Temp.	Sal.	Fq.	Pl.
29 V	60° 13'	4° 24' E.	8,35	33,32	r	Ns Tp
29 V	61° 40'	4° 20' E.	7,05	33,47	r	Ns Tp
30 V	63° 52'	6° 5' E.	8	34,53	r	Tp Ns
31 VIII	76° 12'	12° 18' E.	6,26	35,15	r	S
3 IX	74° 42'	16° 42' E.	7,24	35,17	r	T (S)
4 IX	72° 43'	18° 43' E.	8,8	35,01	+	Tp Ns
4 IX	72° 29'	18° 48' E.	8,87	35,04	r	Tp Ns
5 IX	71° 14'	19° 38' E.	9,40	34,92	r	Tp Ns
6 IX	70° 33'	20° 32' E.	9,87	34,41	r	Tp Ns

Oithona plumifera BAIRD.

Surface: 9 VI. Lat. N. 70° 59'. Long. E. 20° 43'. Temp. 7,15. Sal. 34,83. Fq. rr.
Pl. C (S).

O. similis CLAUS.

Surface:

Date	Lat. N.	Long.	Temp.	Sal.	Fq.	Pl.	Date	Lat. N.	Long.	Temp.	Sal.	Fq.	Pl.
27 V	57° 50'	6° E.	6,70	33,69	c	Tp Ns	25 VIII	70° 53'	11° 22' E.	2,77	33,75	+	C (S) Ng
30 VII	76° 12'	0° 17' W.	4,59	34,53	+	C	28 VIII	78° 23'	10° 23' E.	6,06	34,94	+	T
1 VIII	76° 36'	12° 8' E.	7,38	35,12	+	C T	29 VIII	77° 38'	11° 40' E.	6	34,89	r	T S
3 VIII	77° 46'	26° 18' E.	1,23	30,98	+	C (Ng)	29 VIII	77° 23'	10° 53' E.	5,55	35,08	r	T S
16 VIII	78° 27'	32° 30' E.	1,52	33,46	+	(C) Ng	30 VIII	76° 45'	8° 45' E.	5,84	34,92	c	S
19 VIII	80° 27'	30° 25' E.	−0,30	32,08	r	(Ng)	31 VIII	76° 27'	10° 43' E.	5,85	35,08	r	S
21 VIII	80° 31'	18° 50' E.	2,42	33,93	r	Ng T	31 VIII	76° 12'	12° 18' E.	6,26	35,15	c	S
24 VIII	80° 8'	16° 32' E.	3,44	33,59	r	(Ng)	1 IX	76° 2'	13° 6' E.	6,61	35,13	c	S T

Date.	Lat. N.	Long.	Temp.	Sal.	Fq.	Pl.
2 IX	75°50′	15°32′ E.	5,32	35,01	c	S T
2 IX	75°24′	16°47′ E	5,64	35,12	+	T (s)
3 IX	74°12′	16°42′ E.	7,24	35,17	c	T (S)
1 IX	73°36′	18°50′ E.	7,06	35,03	c	S (Ns)
4 IX	72°43′	18°13′ E.	8,8	35,01	+	Tp Ns
4 IX	72°29′	18°48′ E.	8,87	35,04	+	Tp Ns
5 IX	71°57′	19° E.	9,08	31,96	cc	Tp (Ns)
5 IX	71°14′	19°38′ E.	9,40	34,92	cc	Tp (Ns)

Oncæa minuta GIESBR.

Surface:

Date	Lat. N.	Long.	Temp.	Sal.	Fq.	Pl.
29 VIII	77°38′	11°40′ E.	6	34,89	+	T S
29 VIII	77°23′	10°53′ E.	5,58	35,03	>	T s
31 VIII	76°12′	12°18′ E.	6,26	35,15	r	S
4 IX	72°13′	18°43′ E.	8,8	35,01	r	Tp Ns
5 IX	71°57′	19° E.	9,08	34,96	,	Tp (Ns)

Habitat: Mediterranean (GIESBR.). Eastern Atlantic: in 1898 March to May the Azores to Bretagne, west of Bergen and Lofoten; in July: Lat. N. 65°. Long. E. 1°—6°.

Pseudocalanus elongatus (BOECK).

Surface:

Date.	Lat. N.	Long.	Temp.	Sal.	Fq.	Pl.
29 V	61°10′	4°20′ E.	7,05	33,47	+	Ns Tp
25 VIII	79°53′	11°22′ E.	2,77	33,75	r	C (S) Ng

Temora longicornis (O. F. MÜLL.).

Surface:

Date.	Lat. N	Long.	Temp.	Sal.	Fq.	Pl.
27 V	57°50′	6′ E.	8,70	33,69	r	Tp Ns
28 V	58°41′	4°34′ E.	8,30	33,04	+	Ns Tp
29 V	60°13′	4°24′ E.	8,35	33,32	c	Ns Tp
29 V	61°40′	4°20′ E.	7,05	33,47	r	Ns Tp
30 V	62°11′	5′ E.	7,47	33,12	r	Ns Tp
30 V	63°53′	6°5′ E.	8	34,55	r	Tp Ns

Ciliata.

Cyttarocylis denticulata (Ehb.). Brandt (Bibl. Zool. 1896) has some years ago split the *Tintinnus denticulatus* of Eurenberg in several new species, which, however, seem to me to be mere varieties. But as it is of a certain importance for hydrography to distinguish also races I have tried to keep the forms separate. Around Spitzbergen was found, besides, a new variety *obtusa* (Aurivillius), which differs from var. *gigantea* by the apical end being rounded.

a. *typical C. denticulata.*

Surface:

Date.	Lat. N.	Long.	Temp.	Sal.	Fq.	Pl.
28 V	56° 14'	4° 40' E.	8,8	31,83	r	Ns Tp
30 V	63° 52'	6° 5' E.	8	34,53	+	Tp Ns
31 V	65° 47'	9° 10' E.	9,01	34,67	r	Ns Tp
3 VIII	77° 46'	26° 18' E.	1,23	30,98	r	(Ng)
15 VIII	77° 48'	32° 53' E.	1,55	33,20	r	(C)
15 VIII	78° 38'	34° 30' E.	1,52	34,30	r	c
16 VIII	78° 27'	32° 30' E.	1,52	33,46	r	Ng (C)
29 VIII	77° 38'	11° 40' E.	6	34,89	r	T S
31 VIII	76° 12'	12° 18' E.	6,26	35,15	r	S
1 IX	76° 2'	13° 8' E.	6,61	35,18	r	T S
2 IX	75° 24'	16° 47' E.	5,64	35,12	c	T(S)
4 IX	73° 36'	18° 50' E.	7,06	35,03	r	S (Ns)

b. *Var. edentula* (C. edentula Brandt).

Surface:

Date.	Lat. N.	Long.	Temp.	Sal.	Fq.	Pl.
26 VII	77° 53'	5° 3' E.	4,78	34,57	r	(C)
30 VII	78° 12'	0° 17' W.	4,59	34,53	c	(C)
31 VII	77° 14'	6° 34' E.	5,35	34,77	cc	S
29 VIII	77° 38'	11° 40' E.	6	34,89	r	S T
29 VIII	77° 23'	10° 53' E.	5,55	35,08	c	S T
1 IX	76° 2'	13° 8' E.	6,61	35,13	c	S T

c. *Var. gigantea* (C. gigantea Brandt).

Surface:

Date.	Lat. N.	Long.	Temp.	Sal.	Fq.	Pl.
29 V	61° 40'	4° 20' E.	7,05	33,47	r ×	Ns Tp
30 V	62° 41'	5° E.	7,47	33,12	r ×	Ns Tp
30 V	63° 13'	5° 15' E.	8,17	34,53	r ×	Tp Ns
31 V	65° 19'	8° 20' E.	8,35	35,34	r ×	?

Date.	Lat. N.	Long.	Temp.	Sal.	Fq.	Pl.	Date.	Lat. N.	Long.	Temp.	Sal.	Fq.	Pl.
31 V	65° 34'	8° 45' E.	8,83	35,00	,	Ns T	20 VIII	80° 45'	26° 40' E.	0,15	32,20	r	(Ng)
1 VI	66° 42'	10° 30' E.	8,53	34,89	r ×	T Tp Ns	26 VIII	78° 23'	10° 23' E.	6,96	34,94	r	T(Ng)
2 VI	68° 30'	13° 10' E.	7,55	34,33	r	Ns C	29 VIII	77° 38'	11° 40' E.	6	34,89	r	T S
11 VI	72° 10'	21° 46' E.	5,53	35,25	r ×	(C T)	31 VIII	76° 27'	10° 43' E.	5,35	35,03	r ×	S
12 VI	78° 40'	22° 40' E.	2,10	35,05	,	C	1 IX	76° 2'	13° 8' E.	6,61	35,13	r	T S
23 VI	77° 15'	27° 10' E.	0,97	33,15	r	(C)	2 IX	75° 50'	15° 32' E.	5,52	35,01	r ×	S T
28 VII	77° 52'	3° 5' W.	3,63	34,36	+	C	2 IX	75° 24'	16° 47' E.	5,64	35,12	c	T(S)
3 VIII	77° 46'	26° 18' E.	1,23	30,98	c	—	5 IX	71° 14'	19° 38' E.	9,40	34,92	c	Tp Ns

d. *Var. media* (C. media Brandt).

Surface:

Date.	Lat. N.	Long.	Temp.	Sal.	Fq.	Pl.	Date.	Lat. N.	Long.	Temp.	Sal.	Fq.	Pl.
30 V	62° 41'	5° E.	7,17	33,12	rr	Ns Tp	29 VIII	77° 38'	11° 40' E.	6	34,89	c	T S
26 VII	78° 13'	7° 30' E.	5,34	34,89	r	—	29 VIII	77° 28'	10° 53' E.	5,55	35,03	r	T S
26 VII	77° 53'	5° 3' E.	4,78	34,57	r	(C)	30 VIII	77°	8° 3' E.	5,65	35,03	r	T S
30 VII	76° 12'	0° 17' W.	4,59	34,53	+	C	30 VIII	76° 45'	8° 45' E.	5,34	34,92	r ×	S
3 VIII	77° 3'	23° 35' E.	3,94	34,45	r	(C)	31 VIII	76° 27'	10° 43' E.	5,35	35,03	r	S
15 VIII	77° 48'	32° 53' E.	1,55	33,20	r	(C)	31 VIII	76° 12'	12° 18' E.	6,20	35,15	+	S
16 VIII	78° 27'	32° 30' E.	1,52	33,46	,	Ng (C)	2 IX	75° 50'	15° 32' E.	5,52	35,01	r	S T
20 VIII	81° 8'	23° 35' E.	0,71	32,84	r	Ng	2 IX	75° 24'	16° 47' E.	5,64	35,12	c	T(S)
21 VIII	80° 31'	16° 50' E.	2,42	33,93	,	Ng T	3 IX	74° 43'	16° 42' E.	7,24	35,17	r	T(S)
25 VIII	79° 53'	11° 22' E.	2,77	33,75	+	C (S) Ng	4 IX	73° 36'	18° 50' E.	7,06	35,03	r	S (Ns)
27 VIII	79° 58'	9° 35' E.	4,53	34,53	r	T	4 IX	72° 43'	18° 43' E.	8,8	35,01	r	Tp Ns
28 VIII	78° 23'	10° 23' E.	6,08	34,94	c	T	5 IX	71° 57'	19' E.	9,08	34,96	,	Tp (Ns)

e. *Var. obtusa* Auriv.

Surface:

Date.	Lat. N.	Long.	Temp.	Sal.	Fq.	Pl.
21 VI	76° 27'	25° 55' E.	0,24	33,68	r	(C)
3 VIII	77° 46'	26° 18' E.	1,23	30,98	r	(C)
4 VIII	78° 18'	28° E.	2,12	33,01	r	Ng C
15 VIII	77° 48'	32° 53' E	1,55	33,20	r	(C)
15 VIII	78° 36'	34° 30' E.	1,52	33,21	+	C
16 VIII	78° 27'	32° 30' R.	1,52	33,46	c	Ng C
18 VIII	79° 55'	32° 10' E.	—0,58	33,21	r	Ng C
19 VIII	80° 27'	30° 15' E.	—0,90	32,03	+	Ng

Fungella arctica Cl. N. Sp. By this name I propose to distinguish, provisionally, an organism, which, as I believe, belongs to the ciliate infusoria, but differs considerably from all known forms. Having had no opportunity of examining living specimens I am, at present, unable to characterize the new genus sufficiently. It seems to be nearest allied to the problematic Baltic form, designed by Hensen as »Sternhaarstatoblasten» and of which I have found some specimens in one of the hauls from Spitzbergen.

The Fig. 1, Pl. I represents on empty shell, which is very hyaline and structureless. The animal inhabits the central ovate cavity, which on alcohol-preserved specimens was quite filled by a granular mass.

Diam.: 0,13; height 0,096; diam. of the opening 0,025 mm.
Surface: 20. VIII. 80° 8' N. 16° 32' E. Temp. 3,44. Sal. 33,50.
Habitat: found recently on the coasts of Denmark, Holland and England.

Ptychocylis acuta BRANDT.

Surface:

Date.	Lat. N.	Long.	Temp.	Sal.	Fq.	Pl.
1 VI	66° 42'	10° 30' E.	8,53	34,69	r ×	T Tp Ns
26 VIII	78° 23'	10° 23' E.	6,06	34,94	+	$T(Ng)$
29 VIII	77° 33'	11° 40' E.	6	34,89	r	ST
31 VIII	76° 12'	12° 18' E.	6,26	35,15	c	S
1 IX	76° 2'	13° 8' E.	6,61	35,13	c	ST
2 IX	75° 50'	15° 32' E.	5,52	35,01	+	ST
2 IX	75° 24'	16° 47' E.	5,64	35,12	+	$T(S)$
3 IX	74° 42'	16° 42' E.	7,24	35,17	c	$T(S)$
4 IX	73° 36'	18° 50' E.	7,06	35,03	r	$S(Ns)$
4 IX	72° 43'	18° 43' E.	8,6	35,01	+	Tp Ns
5 IX	71° 57'	19° E.	9,08	34,96	r	$Tp(Ns)$
5 IX	71° 14'	19° 38' E.	9,40	34,92	r	Tp Ns

As the planktontype Ns is derived from T, it is from the above dates evident that this species belongs to the trichotype.

P. obtusa BRANDT. Being unable to distinguish between *P. obtusa* and *P. Drygalskii* BRANDT, I believe that the above name comprises both.

Surface:

Date.	Lat. N.	Long.	Temp.	Sal.	Fq.	Pl.	Date.	Lat. N.	Long.	Temp.	Sal.	Fq.	Pl.
12 VI	73° 40'	22° 40' E.	2,40	35,05	r	C	20 VIII	80° 45'	26° 40' E.	0,13	32,20	r	Ng
20 VI	74° 53'	20° 17' E.	0,16	34,76	r	$C(Ng)$	20 VIII	81° 6'	23° 35' E.	0,71	32,84	o	Ng
21 VI	76° 27'	25° 55' E.	0,24	33,68	r	(C)	21 VIII	80° 31'	18° 50' E.	2,42	33,93	+	Ng T
23 VI	77° 16'	27° 10' E.	0,97	33,15	+	(C)	24 VIII	80° 8'	16° 32' E.	3,44	33,59	r	(Ng)
25 VI	76° 34'	17° 24' E.	0,6	33,80	+	—	25 VIII	79° 53'	11° 22' E.	2,77	33,75	+	$C(S) Ng$
26 VII	78° 13'	7° 30' E.	5,34	34,89	r	—	27 VIII	79° 56'	9° 35' E.	4,56	34,53	r	T
3 VIII	77° 46'	26° 18' E.	1,23	30,98	r	$(C Ng)$	28 VIII	78° 23'	10° 23' E.	6,06	34,93	r	$T(Ng)$
4 VIII	78° 18'	28° E.	2,12	33,01	+	$Ng C$	29 VIII	77° 38'	11° 40' E.	6	34,89	r	TC
15 VIII	77° 48'	32° 53' E.	1,55	33,20	+	(C)	29 VIII	77° 23'	10° 53' E.	5,55	35,03	c	TS
15 VIII	78° 38'	34° 30' E.	1,52	33,21	+	C	30 VIII	77°	8° 3' E.	5,65	35,08	r	S
16 VIII	78° 27'	32° 30' E.	1,52	33,46	c	$Ng C$	30 VIII	76° 45'	6° 45' E.	5,34	34,92	r	S
18 VIII	79° 55'	32° 10' E.	—0,58	33,21	r	$Ng C$	31 VIII	76° 27'	10° 43' E.	5,35	35,08	+ ×	S
19 VIII	80° 27'	30° 15' E.	—0,90	32,03	c	Ng	3 IX	74° 42'	16° 42' E.	7,24	35,17	r	$T(S)$
20 VIII	81° 14'	22° 50' E.	0,58	33,42	+	T							

This species is evidently an arctic neritic form, characterizing the type Ng.

Tintinnus? calyptra CL. N. sp. Shell irregularly conical. Opening not denticulate. End closed. Some few, obliquely transverse lines are visible, especially towards the opening. Structure: small, rounded alveoli, arranged nearly quincuncially.

Diam.: 0,04; height 0,09 mm. Pl. I, fig. 2.
Very rare: 31. VIII. 76° 27' N. 10° 43' E. Temp. 5,35. Sal. 35,03. Pl. *S*.

T. minutus BRANDT. As I have seen no figure of this species I am somewhat uncertain about the identification. The form which I suppose to be *T. minutus* is figured in the Pl. I, fig. 3 and differs from *T. gracilis* BRANDT in the less close teeth only, so that the above name probably comprises both. Diam. 0,03; height 0,05 mm.

Surface:

Date.	Lat. N.	Long.	Temp.	Sal.	Fq.	Pl.
3 VIII	77° 46'	26° 18' E.	1.23	30,98	r	(C Ng)
15 VIII	78° 38'	34° 30' E.	1,52	33,21	+	C
21 VIII	80° 31'	18° 50' E.	2,42	33,93	r	Ng T
25 VIII	79° 58'	11° 22' E.	2,77	33,75	r	C (s) Ng
28 VIII	78° 23'	10° 23' E.	6,06	34,94	r	T (Ng)
20 VIII	77° 38'	11° 40' E.	6	34,89	+	T S
29 VIII	77° 23'	10° 53' E.	5,55	35,03	+	T s
31 VIII	76° 27'	10° 43' E.	5,35	35,03	r	s
1 IX	76° 2'	13° 8' E.	6,61	35,13	+	S T
3 IX	75° 50'	15° 32' E.	5,52	35,01	r ×	s T

T.? pellucidus CL. N. sp. Shell a thin, structureless, irregular tube, which towards the wider opening has a number of close and fine, transverse lines. No foreign agglutinated bodies.

Diam. 0,04; height 0,24 mm. Pl. I, fig. 4.

Surface:

Date.	Lat. N.	Long.	Temp.	Sal.	Fq.	Pl.
20 VIII	81° 14'	22° 50' E.	1,18	33,42	r	T
20 VIII	81° 8'	23° 35' E.	0,71	32,84	r	(Ng)
21 VIII	80° 31'	18° 50' E.	2,42	33,93	r	Ng T
27 VIII	79° 58'	9° 35' E.	4,58	34,53	r	T

T. secatus BRANDT.

Surface:

Date.	Lat. N.	Long.	Temp.	Sal.	Fq.	Pl.	Date.	Lat. N.	Long.	Temp	Sal.	Fq.	Pl.
21 VIII	80° 31'	18° 50' E.	2,42	33,93	r	Ng T	30 VIII	77°	8° 3' E.	5,65	35,03	r	s
25 VIII	79° 58'	11° 22' E.	2,77	33,75	r	C (s) Ng	31 VIII	76° 27'	10° 43' E.	5,35	35,03	r	s
29 VIII	77° 38'	11° 40' E.	6	34,89	rr	S T	1 IX	76° 2'	13° 8' E.	6,61	35,13	r	S T
29 VIII	77° 23'	10° 53' E.	5,55	35,03	+	T S							

Cystoflagellata.

Noctiluca miliaris SURIRAY.
26. V. Lat. N. 58° 41'. Long E. 4° 34'. Temp. 8,30. Sal. 33,04. Fq. *rr*. Pl. *Tp*.

Silicoflagellata.

Dictyocha speculum EHB.

Surface:

Date.	Lat. N.	Long.	Temp.	Sal.	Fq.	Pl.
31 VIII	76° 27'	10° 43' E.	5,35	35,03	*r*	*S*
1 IX	76° 2'	13° 8' E.	6,61	35,13	*rr*	*S T*

Radiolaria.

Acanthochiasma Krohnii HKL.
5. IX. Lat. N. 71° 50'. Long E. 19° 2'. Haul 250—0 m. Fq. *rr*. Pl. *S*.

Acanthocorys umbellifera HKL.

Deep-sea hauls:

Date.	Lat. N.	Long.	Depth.	Fq.	Pl.
1 VIII	76° 36'	12° 13' E.	500—0 m.	*r*	*T S*
27 VIII	79° 58'	9° 35' E.	400—0 »	*r*	*C N*
1 IX	75° 50'	15° 25' E.	325—0 »	*r*	*S*
5 IX	71° 50'	19° 2' E.	230—0 »	*r*	*S*

Habitat Mediterranean (HKL.). Styliplankton of the warmer Atlantic. Färöe Channel (CL.).

Acanthometron elasticum HKL.
Surface: 31. VIII. Lat. N 76° 27'. Long E. 10° 43'. Temp. 5,35. Sal. 35,03. Fq. *rr*. Pl. *S*.

A. quadrifolium (HKL.). — As I am unable to distinguish between *Acanthonia quadrifolia* and *Acanthometron catervatum* HKL. the above name may comprise both. Also *Acanthometron siculum* does not seem to be anything but a larger and stouter form of the same species. In most samples with *A. quadrifol*. I have seen *Acanthostauros pallidus* (CLAP. & LACHM.), which seems to me not to be anything but a younger form of

Acanthometron quadrifolium, as transitional forms exist. I therefore include this form in *A. quadrifolium*.

Surface:

Date.	Lat. N	Long.	Temp.	Sal.	Fq.	Pl.
4 IX	72°43′	18°43′ E.	8,8	35,01	r	Tp Ns
5 IX	71°57′	19° E.	9,08	34,96	c	Tp (Ns)
5 IX	71°14′	19°38′ E.	9,40	31,92	c	Tp Ns
6 IX	70°23′	20°32′ E.	9,37	34,41	+	Tp Ns

Deep-sea hauls:

Date.	Lat. N.	Long.	Depth.	Fq.	Pl.
26–27 VII	77°39′	1°18′ E.	500—0 m.	r	T N
1 IX	75°50′	15°25′ E.	325—0 »	,	N

Acanthonia Mülleri H<small>KL</small>.

Surface:

Date.	Lat. N.	Long.	Temp.	Sal.	Fq.	Pl.
2 IX	75°50′	15°32 E.	5,52	35,01	,	N T
5 IX	71°57′	19° E.	9,08	34,96	+	Tp (Ns)

Habitat: Mediterranean (H<small>KL</small>.). — Styliplankton of the warmer Atlantic (C<small>L</small>.).

Actinomma boreale C<small>L</small>. N. sp.

a. *Primordial shell.* Thick walled, 0,06 mm. in diameter, with rounded, regular pores (0,003 to 0,005 mm. in diameter), two to three times broader than the bars, four on the radius. Spines in variable number, with triangular and forked apophyses half way to the apex. — Pl. I, fig. 5 *a*.

b. *Secundary (Haliomma-)shell.* Thick walled, 0,08 mm. in diameter, with rounded pores of unequal size (0,01 to 0,02 mm. in diameter), three to four on the radius. Bars 0,002 to 0,003 mm. thick. Spines in variable number, stout shorter than the radius, scattered at intervals. — Resembles *Haliomma beroes*. — Fig.: Pl. I, f. 5 *b*.

c. *Tertiary (Actinomma-)shell.* Thin walled, 0,1 to 0,12 mm. in diameter, with numerous, small (0,002 to 0,007 mm. in diameter), irregular rounded pores. Bars as broad as the pores. Spines numerous, scattered, half as long as the radius. — Fig.: Pl. I, f. 5 *c; d* structure.

Deep-sea hauls:

Date.	Lat. N.	Long.	Depth.	Fq.	Pl.
29–30 VII	78°13′	2°58′ W.	2,600—0 m.	,	N C
1 VIII	76°36′	12°13′ E.	500—0 »	r	T N
27 VIII	79°58′	9°35′ E.	400—0 »	r	N C
1 IX	75°50′	15°25′ E.	325—0 »	r	N
5 IX	71°50′	19° 2 E.	230—0 »	r	N

Artrostrobus annulatus (BAIL.) HKL. Pl. 1. f. 6.

Deep-sea hauls:

Date.	Lat. N.	Long.	Depth.	Fq.	Pl.
29—30 VII	78° 13'	2° 58' W.	2,600—0 m.	r	C S
1 VIII	76° 36'	12° 13' E.	500—0 »	r	T S

Habitat: Kamtschatka, Greenland.

Aulacantha lævissima HKL. As there exists no figure of this species in HAECKEL's monograph, I am somewhat uncertain about the identification. Length of radial tubes about 1 mm. breadth 0,0012—0,0015 mm.; length of tangential tubes about 0,18 mm. — Pl. I, fig. 7 a radial b tangential tubes.

Deep-sea haul: 29—30 VIII. Lat. N. 78° 13'. Long W. 2° 58'. 2,600—0 m. Fq. + — (Fragments).
Habitat: Färöe Channel.

Aulodendron antarcticum HKL. Detached spines perfectly agreeing with the figures in HAECKEL's monograph.

Deep-sea haul: 29—30 VII. Lat. N. 76° 13'. Long. W. 2° 58'. Fq. r.
Habitat: Kerguelen.

Auloscena spectabilis HKL. Fragments exactly agreeing with the figures in HAECKEL's monograph.

Deep-sea haul: 29—30 VII. Lat. N. 76° 13'. Long. W. 2° 58'. Fq. +.
Habitat: Antarctic Ocean (surface).

Beroetta melo CL. N. Sp. *Gen. char.* Family *Challengerida*. Shell without inner prominent tube of the mouth, with apical thoot but without marginal spines. Mouth simple, without peristome. Shell longitudinally furrowed. — *Sp. char.* Shell ovate. Length 0,09 mm. Breadth 0,05 mm. Longitudinal furrows 3 in 0,01 mm. Mouth 0,02 mm. in diameter.

Very rare in the deep-sea gathering: 29—30 VII. Lat. N. 78° 13'. Long. W. 2° 58. 2,600—0 m.
Pl. I, f. 8.

Botryopyle setosa CL. N. S. Length 0,085 mm. Breadth 0,05 mm. Cephalis trilobate, with rounded, irregular pores and some scattered setæ. Thorax twice as long as the cephalis, with very irregular pores of different size.

Pl. I, f. 10 a; b Cephalis from below, showing the septum.

Deep-sea hauls:

Date.	Lat. N.	Long.	Depth.	Fq.	Pl.
29—30 VII	78° 13'	2° 58' W.	500—0 m.	r	S C
1 VIII	76° 36'	12° 13' E.	500—0 »	r	T S
27 VIII	79° 58'	9° 35' E.	400—0 »	r	C S
1 IX	75° 50'	15° 25' E.	325—0 »	r	S

Challengeria Harstonii J. MURRAY.

Deep-sea hauls:

Date.	Lat. N.	Long.	Depth.	Fq.	Pl.
29—30 VIII	78° 13'	2° 58' W.	2,600—0 m.	r	S C
27 VIII	79° 58'	9° 35' E.	400—0 »	r	S C
1 IX	75° 50'	15° 25' E.	325—0 »	r	S

Habitat: The abysmal depths east of Japan.

C. tridens HKL.

Surface:

Date.	Lat. N.	Long.	Temp.	Sal.	Fq.	Pl.
29 VIII	77° 38'	13° 40' E.	6	34,89	r	T S
1 IX	76° 2'	13° 8' E.	6,01	35,18	r	T S

Deep-sea hauls:

Date.	Lat. N.	Long.	Depth.	Fq.	Pl.
29—30 VIII	78° 13'	2° 58' W.	2,600—0 m.	r	C S
27 VIII	79° 58'	9° 35' E.	400—0 »	r	C S
1 IX	75° 50'	15° 25' E.	325—0 »	r	S
5 IX	71° 50'	19° 2' E.	230—0 »	r	S

Habitat: Färöe Channel.

Challengeron Nathorstii CL. N. sp. Shell ovate to subspherical, with a single spine at the apical pole, as long as the radius of the shell or longer. Diameter of the mouth half as long as the diameter of the shell. Structure: regular hexagonal alveoli, quincuncially arranged in obliquely decussating rows (3 in 0,01 mm.). Peristome finely punctate, with two long and pointed, hollow, almost parallel horns, and below each of them a triangular or ovate hole.

Diameter of the shell 0,06 to 0,08 mm. Pl. I, f. 9 *a*. Fig. 9 *b* structure.
The nearest relative is *C. diodon* from the south-eastern Pacific Ocean.

Deep-sea hauls:

Date.	Lat. N.	Long.	Depth.	Fq.	Pl.
27 VIII	79° 58'	9° 35' E.	400—0 m.	rr	S C
5 IX	71° 50'	19° 2' E.	230—0 »	rr	S

Habitat: Surface, 64° 25' N.; 11° 50' W. 10th March 1899.

Collozoum inerme (J. MÜLL.).

Surface:

Date.	Lat. N.	Long.	Temp.	Sal.	Fq.	Pl.
9 VI	70° 54'	20° 43' E.	7,15	34,83	r	C (S)
10 VI	71° 10'	21° 31' E.	6,71	35,20	c	C S
10 VI	71° 42'	22° 35' E.	6,40	35,15	r	T C

Habitat: Cosmopolitan, common in all warmer seas (Mediterranean, Atlantic, Indian and Pacific) HÆCKEL.
— Not rare in the styliplankton of the eastern Atlantic (CL.).

Cromyomma zonaster (EHB). Thick walled and obscure, 0,11 mm. in diameter, densely covered with thin, flexible, radial spines, as long as the radius. Pores rounded 0,005 to 0,007 mm. in diameter; bars 0,003 to 0,005 mm. broad.

Deep-sea haul: 5. IX. Lat. N. 71° 50'. Long. E. 19° 2'. Fq. rr. Pl. S.
Habitat: Greenland, abysmal.

Dictyocephalus sp. In one of the deep-sea hauls was found one specimen (Pl. II, fig. 1) which perhaps may be *D. obtusus* or *Lophophœna obtusa* EHB. Micrg. XXII, f. 40.

Dictyophimus gracilipes BAIL. *Cephalis* hemispherical, with a single stout horn of variable length. Pores rounded. *Thorax* a three-sided smooth pyramide, with three decurrent ribs, prolonged in long, smooth three-sided feet. Pores rounded, irregular, decreasing in size towards the cephalis.

Cephalis 0,02 mm. long; horn 0,04—0,05 mm. Thorax 0,05 mm. long and 0,07 mm. broad. Pl. II, fig. 2.

Deep-sea hauls:

Date.	Lat. N.	Long.	Depth.	Fq.	Pl.
29—30 VII	78° 13'	2° 58' W.	2,600—0 m.	r	C S
1 VIII	76° 36'	12° 13' E.	500—0 »	r	T S
27 VIII	79° 58'	9° 35' E.	400—0 »	r	C S
1 IX	75° 50'	15° 25' E.	325—0 »	r	S

Habitat: Kamtschatka and the north Pacific Ocean.

Euphysetta Nathorstii CL. N. sp. Shell ovate, with a single spine on the apical pole. Structure double: coarser longitudinal (9 in 0,01 mm.) and transverse (8 to 9 in 0,01 mm.) faint ribs crossing each other at right angles and, besides, very small puncta arranged in obliquely decussating rows (17 in 0,01 mm.). Peristome short and wide, with four slender articulate teeth, three of the same length but the fourth much longer. From the middle of the fourth tooth there issues in the middle a small spine.

Length 0,06 mm. Breadth 0,04 mm. Pl. II, fig. 3.
Deep-sea haul: 29—30 VII. Lat. N. 78° 13'. Long. W. 2° 58'. Fq. rr. Depth 2,600—0 m.
Of the genus Euphysetta three species only are known, all from the tropical and southern Atlantic.

Euscenium tricolpium HKL.
Deep-sea haul: 29—30 VII. Lat. N. 78° 13'. Long. W. 2° 58'. Fq. rr. Depth 2,600—0 m.
Habitat: Central Pacific Ocean, abysmal (HKL.). — Northern Atlantic, between Shetlands and Norway, surface (March 1898 CL.).

Gazelletta sp.
Fragments of the feet (smooth) were found in the deep-sea haul: 29—30 VII. Lat. N. 78° 13'. Long. W. 2° 58'. Depth 2,600—0 m.

Heliosphæra actinota HKL.
One small specimen (Diam. 0,06 mm. Pores three on the radius, 0,013 mm. broad) in the deep-sea haul 29—30 VII. Lat. N. 78° 13'. Long. W. 2° 58'. 2,600—0 m.
Habitat: Mediterranean, Canaries, Azores (HKL.).

Hexadoras borealis CL. N. sp.

Primordial shell: irregularly spherical, 0,03 to 0,04 mm. in diameter, with irregular, rounded or polygonal pores, 2 to 3 on the radius, and thin bars. Spines six, exceptionally more, strong, with triangular apophyses in the middle. Pl. II, fig. 4 a.

Outer shell: a rounded or octahedric, more or less intricate net-work of anastomosing, silicious threads, issuing from the proximal edges of the spines. Spines usually six (rarely as in *Rhizoplegma* 8 to 10) strong, three-sided slightly spirally twisted, with elegantly aculeate, winged edges.

Diam. 0,12 to 0,16 mm. Spines 0,1 mm. Pl. II, fig. 4 b, c.

Deep-sea hauls:

Date.	Lat. N.	Long.	Depth.	Fq.	Pl.
1 VIII	76° 36'	12° 13' E.	500—0 m.	r	T S
27 VIII	79° 58'	9° 35' E.	400—0 »	r	C S
5 IX	71° 50'	19° 2' E.	230—0 »	r	S

Habitat: North Atlantic, between Shetlands and Norway, surface, March 1898 (CL.).

Litholophus ligurinus HKL. (*L. arcticus* AURIV.).

Surface:

Date.	Lat. N.	Long.	Temp.	Sal.	Fq.	Pl.
26 VII	78° 13'	7° 30' E.	5,31	34,89	r	—
27 VIII	79° 58'	9° 35' E.	4,58	34,53	r	T
29 VIII	77° 23'	10° 58' E.	5,55	35,03	r	S T
31 VIII	76° 27'	10° 43' E.	5,85	35,03	r	S
31 VIII	76° 12'	12° 18' E.	6,26	35,15	r	S

Deep-sea hauls:

Date.	Lat. N.	Long.	Depth.	Fq.	Pl.
26 27 VII	77° 39'	1° 18' E.	100—0 m.	+	T S
27 VIII	79° 58'	9° 35' E.	400—0 »	r	C S

Habitat: Mediterranean, central Pacific Ocean (HKL.).

Lithomitra australis (EHR.)? The shell Pl. II, fig. 5 seems to be the upper joints of Eucyrtidium australe EHR. from the South Polar ice (Microg. 35 A XXI, f. 18). It was found very rarely in the haul 29—30 VII. Lat. N. 78° 13'. Long. W. 2° 58'. 2,600—0 m. Fig. 6, Pl. II represents a nearly related form from the same gathering.

L. lineata (EHR.). Pl. II, fig. 7.

Deep-sea hauls:

Date.	Lat. N.	Long.	Depth.	Fq.	Pl.
29—30 VII	78° 13'	2° 58' W.	2,600—0 m.	r	C S
27 VIII	79° 58'	9° 35' E.	400—0 »	r	C S
5 IX	71° 50'	19° 2' E.	230—0 »	r	S

Habitat: Mediterranean, Atlantic, Indian and Pacific Oceans (HKL.).

Peridium (?) intricatum CL. N. sp. Shell irregularly polyhedral, of a very loose and irregular frame-work with large, polygonal meshes, the apical being the largest. Basal plate with three large meshes of about the same size. Horn short.

Pl. II, fig. 8 *a* and *b* in different foci.
Diameter of the shell 0,08 mm.
Deep-sea haul: 29—30 VII. Lat. N. 78° 13'. Long. W. 2° 58'. 2,600—0 m. One single specimen.

P. (?) laxum CL. N. sp. Shell irregularly polyhedral of a very loose frame-work, with large polygonal and irregular meshes, the apical being the largest. Basal plate with two cardinal and two jugular meshes of about the same size. Horn a fine bristle, half as long as the shell.

Pl. II, fig. 9 *a*, *b* (in different foci).
Diam. of the shell 0,06 mm.
Deep-sea haul: 5. IX. Lat. N. 71° 50'. Long. E. 19° 2'. 230—0 m. One single specimen.

P. (?) minutum CL. N. sp. By this name I denote provisionally a very small shell, which perhaps might be the primordial shell of *Dictyophimus gracilipes* or *Acanthocorys umbellifera*, to which I have not yet succeeded in finding transitional forms. It is represented on the Pl. III, fig. 1 *a*, *b*, *c*, the two latter being the same shell in different foci. — The diameter of the shell 0,03 to 0,04 mm.

Deep-sea hauls:

Date.	Lat. N.	Long.	Depth.	Fq.	Pl.
23—30 VII	78° 13'	2° 58' W.	2,600 –2 m.	r	C N
27 VIII	71° 50'	9° 35' E.	400—0 »	r	C N

Phorticium pylonium HKL. To this variable and cosmopolitan species I refer the shell figured on the Pl. III, fig. 2 *a*, *b*, *c*. The fig. *d* represents the *primordial shell*, which occurs isolated in the deep-sea gatherings and bears a strong resemblance to *Haliomma æquorea* EHB. (Microg. XIX, 51 from Aegina).

Deep-sea hauls:

Date.	Lat. N.	Long.	Depth.	Fq.	Pl.
29—30 VII	78° 13'	2° 58' W.	2,600—0 m.	r	8 C
1 VIII	76° 36'	12° 13' E.	500—0 »	r	T S
27 VIII	79° 58'	9° 35' E.	400—0 »	r	C N
1 IX	75° 50'	15° 25' E.	325—0 »	r	N
5 IX	71° 50'	19° 2' E.	230—0 »	r	N

Plectophora arachnoides (CLAP. & LACHM.) HKL. In this species I include also *Plagiacantha arachnoides* (CLAP. & LACHM.) HKL., which represents the young state. The net-work combining the spines is subject to great variation.

Surface:

Date.	Lat. N.	Long.	Temp.	Sal.	Fq.	Pl.	Date.	Lat. N.	Long.	Temp.	Sal.	Fq.	Pl.
10 VI	71° 10'	21°31' E.	6,71	35,26	r	C S	1 IX	76° 2'	13° 8' E.	6,61	35,13	r	S T
28 VIII	78° 23'	10°23' E.	6,06	34,94	r	T	2 IX	75° 60'	15°32' E.	5,52	35,01	+	S T
29 VIII	77° 38'	11°40' E.	6	34,89	r	T S	2 IX	75° 24'	16°47' E.	5,64	35,12	r	T (S)
30 VIII	77	8° 3' E.	5,65	35,03	r	N	3 IX	74° 42'	16°42' E.	7,24	35,17	r	T (S)
30 VIII	76° 45'	8°45' E.	5,94	34,92	r	S	4 IX	78° 36'	18°50' E.	7,06	35,03	r	S (Ns)
31 VIII	76° 27'	10°43' E.	5,95	35,03	1	S	6 IX	70° 23'	20°32' E.	9,37	34,41	r	Tp (Ns)
31 VIII	76° 12'	12°18' E.	6,26	35,15	r	S							

Deep-sea hauls:

Date.	Lat. N.	Long.	Depth.	Fq.	Pl.
1 VIII	76° 36'	12° 13' E.	500—0 m.	r	T S
27 VIII	79° 58'	9° 35' E.	400—0 »	r	C S
1 IX	75° 50'	15° 25' E.	325—0 »	r	S

Habitat: Coasts of Scotland and Norway. Newfoundland Banks (CL.).

Plectanium (?) simplex CL. N. sp. — Bars thin, cylindrical, each divided at the distal end into three branches, connected by thin threads into a delicate polyhedral network (Diam. 0,06 mm.).

Pl. III, fig. 3.
One single specimen in the haul 29—30 VII. Lat. N. 78° 13'. Long. W. 2° 58'. — 2,600—0 m.

Polypetta holostoma CL. N. sp. — Shell spherical. Structure: triangular alveoli (1,5 in 0,01 mm.) separated by prominent fine crests. At each point, where these crests cross each other, a short, small thorn arises. On the surface of the shell are scattered without order a number of narrow, structure-less, straight or slightly curved tubes, longer around the proboscis, where they are three to four times as long as the diameter of the shell. Proboscis a cylindrical tube, somewhat shorter than the diameter of the shell. The mouth with a narrow, undivided rim.

Diam. 0,09 to 0,1 mm.
Pl. III, fig. 4 *a; b* structure.
Deep-sea haul: 29—30 VII. Lat. N. 78° 13'. Lat. W. 2° 58'. — 2,600—0 m. r.
This species agrees in all respects, except the mouth, with *Polypetta tabulata* HKL. from the abysmal depth of the Indian Ocean.

Pterocorys irregularis CL. N. sp. — Cephalis nearly spherical, with one apical and one lateral horn. Its pores small and indistinct. Thorax with three strong, downwards directed horns, as long as the breadth of the thorax. Pores rounded, as broad as the bars, variable in size (0,002 to 0,008 mm. in diameter) and scattered without order. The upper part of the thorax provided with some few spines. Abdomen not distinctly separated from the thorax. Its pores similar to those of the thorax.

Length of cephalis 0,03, of thorax 0,07 mm., of abdomen 0.04 mm. Breadth of thorax 0,07 mm., of abdomen 0,08 mm.
Pl. IV, fig. 1.
The nearest allied form seems to be *P. columba*.
One specimen in the haul 29—30 VII. Lat. N. 78° 13'. Long. W. 2° 58'. — 2,600—0 m.
Habitat: Between Shetlands and Norway, surface, March 1898.

Sagenoscena penicillata HKL. — Agrees with the description and figures in HÆCKEL'S monograph with the exception that the radial rods have the same thickness as the tangential bars and are shorter than these, characteristics so trifling that I do not consider them sufficient for the distinction of a variety.

This species, known from the abysmal depths of the Antarctic Ocean, was found in fragments in the haul 29—30 VII. Lat. N. 78° 13'. Long. W. 2° 58'. — 2,600—0 m.

Sethoconus galea CL. N. sp. — Shell campanulate or hemispherical, as long as broad (0,12 mm.), with rudimentary cephalis, not distinctly separated from the thorax. One apical spine and several small spines on the thorax. Pores irregularly polygonal, increasing in size from the apex, the largest 0,02 mm. in diameter.
Pl. IV, fig. 3.
Some few specimens in the haul 29—30 VII. Lat. N. 78° 13'. Long. W. 2° 58'. — 2,600—0 m.

Sethoconus tabulatus (EHB.) HKL.
Cephalis 0,013 mm. long. Thorax in length 0,03 mm., in breadth 0,045 mm. Largest pores 0,008 mm. in diameter. Cephalis with one delicate horn and several small bristles.
Pl. IV, fig. 2.
This species found by EHRENBERG in the abysmal depths of the Caribbean sea and by the Challenger Expedition in the abysmal depths between Ascension and Sierra Leone was found in the haul the 29—30 VII. Lat. N. 78° 13'. Long. W. 2° 58'. — 2,600—0 m.

Sethophormis sp.
A fragment of a species resembling *S. rotula* HKL. was found in the haul 29—30 VII. Lat. N. 78° 13'. Long. W. 2° 58'. — 2,600—0 m.

Stichopilium davisianum (EHB.). — Pl. IV, fig. 6.
Several specimens in the deep-sea hauls 29—30 VII. Lat. N. 78° 13'. Long. W. 2° 58'. — 2,600—0 m. and 1 IX. Lat. N. 75° 50'. Long. E. 15° 25'. — 325—0 m.
Habitat: Greenland, abysmal.

Theocalyptra cornuta BAIL.
Length of cephalis 0,02, of thorax 0,08, of abdomen 0,01 mm. Diameter of the opening 0,14 mm. Diam. of the largest pores 0,014 mm.

Deep-sea hauls:

29—30 VII.	Lat. N. 78° 13'.	Long. W. 2° 58'.	Depth 2,600—0 m.	Fq. r.
27 VIII.	» » 79° 58'.	» E. 9° 35'.	» 400—0 »	» r.
1 IX	» » 75° 50'.	» » 15° 25'.	» 325—0 »	» r.

Habitat: Kamtschatka (BAIL.), Greenland (EHB.).

Theocorys borealis CL. N. sp. — Cephalis hemispherical, with a short triangular horn and large, irregular, rounded pores. Thorax pear-shaped, with regular, circular pores, as broad as the bars, quincuncially arranged (4 in 0,01 mm.). Abdomen short, narrower than the thorax, with some few, irregular and scattered pores. Mouth somewhat constricted, sometimes with a hyaline peristome.

Length of cephalis 0,015 mm., of thorax 0,03 mm., of abdomen 0,01 to 0,015 mm. Breadth of thorax 0,045 mm. Diameter of the mouth 0,007 mm.
Pl. III, fig. 5.
Resembles *Sethocorys odysseus* HKL. as to the shape and arrangement of the pores.

Deep-sea hauls:

Date.	Lat. N.	Long.	Depth.	Fq.	Pl.
29—30 VII	78° 13'	2° 58' W.	2,600—0 m.	r	S C
27 VIII	79° 58'	9° 35' E.	400—0 »	r	C.S
1 IX	75° 50'	15° 25' E.	325—0 »	r	N

Trochodiscus echinidiscus HKL.

Diam. of the shell 0,38 mm., of the pores 0,005 to 0,01 mm. Length of spines about a third of the radius.
Pl. IV, fig. 4.
One specimen in the deep-sea haul 29—30 VII. Lat. N. 78° 13'. Long. W. 2° 58'. — 2,600—0 m.
Habitat: Färöe Channel (HKL.).

T. helioides CL. N. sp. — Shell 0,24 mm. in diameter, with rounded pores (0,005 to 0,007 mm. in diameter), twice as broad as the bars. Margin with numerous, about 20, spines, as long as the diameter.

Pl. IV, fig. 5.
Haul 27 VII. Lat. N. 78° 58'. Long. E. 9° 35'. — 400—0 m.

Rhizopoda.

Globigerina bulloides D'ORB.

Surface:

Date.	Lat. N.	Long.	Temp.	Sal.	Fq.	Pl.
29 VIII	77° 38'	11° 40' E.	6	34,89	r	T S
30 VIII	77°	5° 3' E.	5,65	35,03	r	(S)
30 VIII	76° 45'	8° 45' E.	5,34	34,92	r	S
31 VIII	76° 27'	10° 43' E.	5,35	35,03	r	S
31 VIII	76° 12'	12° 18' E.	6,26	35,15	r	S
1 IX	76° 2'	13° 8' E.	6,61	35,13	r	S T
2 IX	75° 50'	15° 32' E.	5,52	35,01	r	S T
3 IX	74° 42'	16° 42' E.	7,24	35,17	r	T (S)
4 IX	72° 43'	18° 43' E.	8,8	35,01	r	Tp Ns
5 IX	71° 57'	19° E.	9,08	34,96	r	Tp (Ns)
5 IX	71° 14'	19° 38' E.	9,40	34,92	r	Tp Ns
6 IX	70° 29'	20° 30' E.	9,27	34,41	r	Tp Ns

Chlorophylleæ.

Halosphæra viridis SCHMITZ.

Surface:

Date.	Lat. N.	Long.	Temp.	Sal.	Fq.	Pl.
27 V	57° 50'	6° E.	8,70	33.60	+	Tp Ns
30 V	63° 13'	5° 15' E.	8,17	34,58	r	Tp Ns
4 IX	72° 43'	16° 43' E.	8,8	35,01	c	Tp Ns
4 IX	72° 29'	16° 48' E.	8,87	35,04	+	Tp Ns
5 IX	71° 57'	19° E.	9,08	34,96	c	Tp (Ns)
5 IX	71° 14'	19° 38' E.	9,40	34,92	+	Tp Ns
6 IX	70° 23'	20° 32' E.	9,37	34,41	r	Tp Ns

Flagellatæ.

Dinobryum pellucidum LEVANDER.

Surface:

Date.	Lat. N.	Long.	Temp.	Sal.	Fq.	Pl.
26 VII	77° 39'	1° 18' E.	5,07	32,22	r	—
28 VII	77° 52'	3° 5' W.	3,63	34,38	c	—
15 VIII	77° 48'	32° 53' E.	1,55	33,20	r	(C)
15 VIII	78° 38'	34° 30' E.	1,52	33,21	+	C
16 VIII	78° 27'	33° 30' E.	1,52	33,46	+	Ng C
18 VIII	79° 55'	32° 10' E.	—0,58	33,21	r	Ng (C)
20 VIII	80° 45'	26° 40' E.	0,13	32,20	r	Ng
21 VIII	80° 31'	18° 50' E.	2,42	33,93	r	Ng T
24 VIII	80° 8'	16° 32' E.	3,44	33,59	+	Ng
25 VIII	79° 53'	11° 22' E.	2,77	33,75	r	C S Ng
27 VIII	79° 58'	9° 35' E.	4,58	34,53	r	T

Phæocystis Pouchetii LAGERH.

Surface:

Date.	Lat. N.	Long.	Temp.	Sal.	Fq.	Pl.
11 VI	73° 3'	23° 28' E.	5,15	35,37	c	C
12 VI	73° 40'	22° 40' E.	2,40	35,05	cc	C
20 VI	74° 53'	20° 17' E.	0,16	34,76	+	C
21 VI	76° 27'	25° 55' E.	0,24	33,68	+	(C)
22 VI	76° 45'	26° E.	0,80	34,07	+	(C)
25 VI	76° 34'	17° 24' E.	0,60	33,80	+	((C))
28 VII	77° 52'	3° 5' W.	3,63	34,38	c	C
21 VIII	80° 31'	18° 50' E.	2,42	33,93	+	Ng T
27 VIII	79° 58'	9° 35' E.	4,58	34,53	+	T

Dinoflagellatæ.

Ceratium furca Duj.

Surface:

Date.	Lat. N.	Long.	Temp.	Sal.	Fq.	Pl.	Date.	Lat. N.	Long.	Temp.	Sal.	Fq.	Pl.
27 V	57° 50'	6° E.	8,70	33,69	+	Tp Ns	31 V	65° 47'	9° 10' E.	9,01	34,67	r	Ns Tp
28 V	58° 14'	4° 40' E.	8,8	31,83	+	Ns Tp	1 VI	66° 42'	10° 30' E.	8,53	34,69	c	T Tp Ns
29 V	60° 13'	4° 24' E.	8,35	33,32	+	Ns Tp	2 VI	68° 30'	13° 10' E.	7,55	34,33	+	Ns C
30 V	62° 41'	5° E.	7,47	33,12	r	Ns Tp	2 VI	68° 49'	13° 50' E.	7,70	34,16	+	C Ns
30 V	63° 13'	5° 15' E.	8,17	34,53	+	Tp Ns	4 IX	72° 43'	18° 43' E.	8,8	35,01	c	Tp Ns
30 V	63° 52'	6° 5' E.	8	34,58	c	Tp Ns	5 IX	71° 57'	19° E.	9,08	34,96	r	Tp (Ns)
31 V	65° 19'	8° 20' E.	8,35	35,34	r	—	5 IX	71° 14'	19° 38' E.	9,40	34,92	c	Tp Ns
31 V	65° 34'	8° 45' E.	8,83	35,00	+	Ns T	6 IX	70° 23'	20° 32' E.	9,37	34,41	c	Tp Ns

C. fusus Duj.

Surface:

Date.	Lat. N.	Long.	Temp.	Sal.	Fq.	Pl.	Date.	Lat. N.	Long.	Temp.	Sal.	Fq.	Pl.
27 V	57° 50'	6° E.	8,70	33,69	+	Tp Ns	31 V	65° 47'	9° 10' E.	9,01	34,67	r	Ns Tp
28 V	58° 14'	4° 40' E.	8,8	31,83	r	Ns Tp	2 VI	68° 49'	13° 50' E.	7,70	34,16	+	C Ns
28 V	58° 41'	4° 34' E.	8,30	33,04	r	Ns Tp	4 IX	73° 36'	18° 50' E.	7,06	35,03	r	S (Ns)
29 V	60° 13'	4° 24' E.	8,35	33,32	r	Ns Tp	4 IX	72° 43'	18° 43' E.	8,8	35,01	r	Tp Ns
30 V	62° 41'	5° E.	7,47	33,12	r	Ns Tp	5 IX	71° 14'	19° 38' E.	9,40	34,92	+	Tp Ns
30 V	63° 13'	5° 15' E.	8,17	34,58	+	Tp Ns	6 IX	70° 23'	20° 32' E.	9,37	34,41	r	Tp Ns
31 V	65° 34'	8° 45' E.	8,83	35,00	r	Ns T							

C. lineatum Ehb. (= C. furca v. baltica Moebius).

This form cannot be considered as a mere variety of *C. furca*, and is always easy to recognize. It belongs to the styliplankton of the warmer Atlantic, both in the East and the West. *C. furca* seems on the contrary to be confined to the east Atlantic.

Surface: 5 IX. Lat. N. 71° 50'. Long. E. 19° 2'. Fq. rr.

C. tripos Nitzsch.

Surface:

Date.	Lat. N.	Long.	Temp.	Sal.	Fq.	Pl.	Date.	Lat. N.	Long.	Temp.	Sal.	Fq.	Pl.
27 V	57° 50'	6° E.	8,70	33,69	+	Tp Ns	31 V	65° 34'	8° 45' E.	8,83	35,00	r	Ns T
28 V	58° 14'	4° 40' E.	8,8	31,83	c	Ns Tp	31 V	65° 47'	9° 10' E.	9,01	34,67	+	Ns Tp
28 V	58° 41'	4° 34' E.	8,30	33,04	c	Ns Tp	1 VI	66° 42'	10° 30' E.	8,53	34,69	c	T Tp Ns
29 V	60° 13'	4° 24' E.	8,35	33,32	c	Ns Tp	4 IX	72° 43'	18° 43' E.	8,8	35,01	+	Tp Ns
29 V	61° 40'	4° 20' E.	7,05	33,47	+	Ns Tp	4 IX	72° 29'	18° 43' E.	8,87	35,04	+	Tp Ns
30 V	62° 41'	5° E.	7,47	33,12	c	Ns Tp	5 IX	71° 57'	19° E.	9,08	34,96	+	Tp (Ns)
30 V	63° 13'	5° 15' E.	8,17	34,53	cc	Tp Ns	5 IX	71° 14'	19° 38' E.	9,40	34,92	c	Tp Ns
30 V	63° 52'	6° 5' E.	8	34,58	c	Tp Ns	6 IX	70° 23'	20° 32' E.	9,37	34,41	+	Tp Ns
31 V	65° 19'	8° 20' E.	8,35	35,34	+	?							

C. tripos var. arctica EHB. — I do not, as Dr. AURIVILLIUS, include under this name also the var. *longipes*, which I find always easy to distinguish from the original form, figured in the Microgeologie and by CLAPARÈDE and LACHMANN. The var. *arctica* occurs frequently, sometimes in immense number, in the Labrador current, in Davis strait and around Spitzbergen (optimum salinity 34 p. m.). It belongs thus to the tricho-plankton chiefly, but occurs also in the sira-plankton. The var. *longipes*, on the contrary, is a more neritic form, which occurs in the spring along the whole Norwegian coast-line, around Scotland and in Skagerak. It belongs to the northern neritic plankton.

Surface:

Date.	Lat. N.	Long.	Temp.	Sal.	Fq.	Pl.	Date.	Lat. N.	Long.	Temp.	Sal.	Fq.	Pl.
10 VI	71°10′	21°31′ E.	6,71	35,20	r	C S	20 VIII	81° 8′	23°35′ E.	0,71	32,84	r	Ng
10 VI	71° 43′	22°35′ E.	6,40	35,15	r	T C S	21 VIII	80° 31′	18°50′ E.	2,42	33,93	c	Ng T
26 VII	78° 13′	7°30′ E.	5,34	34,89	r	—	24 VIII	80° 8′	16°32′ E	3,44	33,59	r	Ng
26 VII	77° 53′	5° 3′ E.	4,78	34,57	r	((C))	25 VIII	79° 53′	11°22′ E.	2,77	33,75	r	C (S) Ny
30 VII	78° 12′	0° 17′ W.	4,59	34,53	+	(C)	29 VIII	77° 38′	11°40′ E.	6	34,89	r	S T
1 VIII	76° 36′	12°8′ E.	7,38	35,12	+	S T	29 VIII	77° 23′	10°53′ E.	5,55	35,03	r	S T
3 VIII	77° 46′	26°18′ E.	1,23	30,98	c	(C Ng)	31 VIII	76° 12′	12°18′ E.	6,20	35,15	r	S
4 VIII	78° 18′	26° E.	2,12	33,01	r	Ng C	1 IX	76° 2′	13° 8′ E.	6,61	35,13	r	S T
15 VIII	78° 38′	34°30′ E.	1,52	33,21	+	C	2 IX	75° 50′	15°32′ E.	5,52	35,01	r	S T
16 VIII	78° 27′	32°30′ E.	1,52	33,46	+	Ng C	2 IX	75° 24′	16°47′ E.	5,64	35,12	r	T (S)
18 VIII	79° 55′	32°10′ E.	— 0,58	33,21	+	Ng C	3 IX	74° 42′	16°42′ E.	7,21	35,17	+	T (S)
20 VIII	81° 14′	22°50′ E.	1,18	33,42	r	T	4 IX	73° 36′	18°50′ E.	7,06	35,03	c	S (Ns)
20 VIII	80° 45′	26°40′ E.	0,13	32,20	r	(Ng)							

C. tripos var. bucephala CL.

Surface:

Date.	Lat. N.	Long.	Temp.	Sal.	Fq.	Pl.
27 V	57° 50′	6° E.	8,70	33,69	r	Tp Ns
5 IX	71° 57′	19° E.	9,08	34,96	r	Tp (Ns)

C. tripos var. horrida CL.

Surface:

Date.	Lat. N.	Long.	Temp.	Sal.	Fq.	Pl.
31 V	65° 19′	8°20′ E.	8,35	35,34	cc	—
31 V	65° 34′	8°45′ E.	8,83	35,00	+	Ns T
2 VI	68° 30′	13°10′ E.	7,55	34,33	c	Ns C
2 VI	68° 49′	13°50′ E.	7,70	34,16	c	C Ns
10 VI	71° 10′	21°31′ E.	6,71	35,20	r	C S
6 IX	70° 23′	20°32′ E.	9,37	34,41	c	Tp Ns

C. tripos var. longipes BAIL.

Surface:

Date.	Lat. N.	Long.	Temp.	Sal.	Fq.	Pl.	Date.	Lat. N.	Long.	Temp.	Sal.	Fq.	Pl.
27 V	57° 50'	6° E.	8,70	33,69	cc	Tp Ns	10 VI	71° 42'	22°35' E.	6,40	35,15	r	T C S
28 V	58° 14'	4°40' E.	8,8	31,83	cc	Ns Tp	15 VIII	77° 48'	32°53' E.	1,55	33,20	r	(C)
28 V	58° 41'	4°34' E.	8,30	33,04	cc	Ns Tp	20 VIII	81° 14'	27°50' E.	1,16	33,42	r	T
29 V	60° 13'	4°24' E.	8,35	33,32	c	Ns Tp	20 VIII	81° 8'	25°35' E.	0,71	32,84	r	Ng
29 V	61° 40'	4°21' E.	7,05	33,47	cc	N. Tp	31 VIII	76° 12'	12°18' E	6,26	35,15	i	S
30 V	62° 41'	5° E.	7,17	33,12	cc	Ns Tp	1 IX	76° 2'	13° 8' E.	6,61	35,13	r	S T
30 V	63° 13'	5°15' E.	8,17	34,53	cc	Tp Ns	2 IX	75° 50'	15°32' E.	5,52	35,01	r	S T
30 V	63° 52'	6° 5' E.	8	34,53	cc	Tp Ns	3 IX	74° 42'	16°42' E.	7,24	35,17	+	T (S)
31 V	65° 34'	8°45' E.	8,83	35,00	cc	Ns T	4 IX	73° 36'	18°50' E.	7,06	35,03	c	S (Ns)
31 V	65° 47'	9°10' E.	9,01	34,67	c	Ns Tp	4 IX	72° 43'	18°43' E.	8,8	35,01	c	Tp Ns
1 VI	66° 42'	10°30' E.	8,53	34,69	c	T Tp Ns	4 IX	72° 29'	18°48' E	8,87	35,04	c	Tp Ns
2 VI	68° 30'	13°10' E.	7,55	34,83	c	Ns C	5 IX	71° 57'	19° E.	9,08	34,96	c	Tp (Ns)
2 VI	68° 49'	13°50' E.	7,70	34,16	c	C Ns	5 IX	71° 14'	19°38' E.	9,40	34,92	c	Tp (Ns)
10 VI	71° 10'	21°31' E.	6,71	35,20	r	C S	6 IX	70° 23'	20°32' E.	9,37	34,41	c	Tp (Ns)

C. tripos var. macroceros EHB.

Surface:

Date.	Lat. N.	Long.	Temp.	Sal.	Fq.	Pl.
27 V	57° 50'	6° E.	8,70	33,69	c	Tp Ns
28 V	58° 14'	4°40' E.	8,8	31,83	r	Ns Tp
28 V	58° 41'	4°34' E.	8,30	33,04	+	Ns Tp
29 V	60° 13'	4°24' E.	8,35	33,32	+	Ns Tp
29 V	61° 40'	4°20' E.	7,05	33,47	r	Ns Tp
30 V	63° 13'	5°15' E.	8,17	34,53	r	Tp Ns
30 V	63° 52'	6° 5' E.	8	34,53	v	Tp Ns
31 V	65° 47'	9°10' E.	9,01	34,67	r	Ns Tp
29 VIII	77° 38'	11°40' E.	6	34,89	rr	T S
4 IX	72° 43'	18°43' E.	8,8	35,01	c	Tp Ns
4 IX	72° 29'	16°48' E.	8,87	35,04	c	Tp Ns
5 IX	71 57'	19° E.	9,08	34,96	ccc	Tp (Ns)
5 IX	71° 14'	19°38' E.	9,40	34,92	c	Tp Ns
6 IX	70° 23'	20°32' E.	9,37	34,41	c	Tp Ns

Dinophysis acuta EHB.

Surface:

Date.	Lat. N.	Long.	Temp.	Sal.	Fq.	Pl.
28 V	58° 14'	4°40' E.	8,8	31,83	r	Ns Tp
29 V	60° 13'	4°24' E.	8,35	33,32	r	Ns Tp
30 V	62° 41'	5° E.	7,17	33,12	r	Ns Tp
30 V	63° 52'	6° 5' E.	8	34,53	r	Tp Ns
25 VIII	79° 53'	11°22' E.	2,77	33,75	r	C (S) Ng
6 IX	70° 23'	20°32' E	9,37	34,41	rr	Tp Ns

D. granulata CL. — Under this name I distinguish a very small form (Pl. IV, fig. 7) remarkable for its coarse structure. It seems to belong to the arctic neritic plankton.

Surface:

Date.	Lat. N.	Long.	Temp.	Sal.	Fq.	Pl.
26 VII	77° 53'	5° 3' E.	4,78	34,57	r	((C))
30 VII	78° 12'	0° 17' W.	4,59	34,58	+	(C)
19 VIII	80° 27'	30° 15' E.	—0,90	32,03	r	Ng
20 VIII	80° 45'	26° 40' E.	0,13	32,20	r	Ng
21 VIII	80° 31'	18° 50' E.	2,42	33,93	r	Ng

D. rotundata. In several gatherings were found specimens, which could be considered as *D. rotundata*, but as I believe that several different forms have been confounded under this name, I leave them out.

Diplopsalis lenticula BERGH.
Deep-sea haul: 27 VII. Lat. N. 79° 58'. Long. E. 9° 35'. — 400—0 m. Rare.

Gonyaulax spinifera CLAP. & LACHM.
Haul: 5 IX. Lat. N. 71° 50'. Long. E. 19° 2'. — 25—0 m. Rare.

Gymnaster pentasterias (EHB.).
Haul: 27 VIII. Lat. N. 79° 58'. Long. E. 9° 35'. — 400—0 m. Rare.

Peridinium depressum (BAIL.). — This form ought to be considered as a distinct species and not as a mere variety of *P. divergens*. The latter belongs to the tropical and temperate Atlantic (desmo-, styli- and triposplankton), the former to the northern and western Atlantic (tricho-, tripos- and northern neritic plankton).

Surface:

Date.	Lat. N.	Long.	Temp.	Sal.	Fq.	Pl.	Date.	Lat. N.	Long.	Temp.	Sal.	Fq.	Pl.
27 V	57° 50'	6° E.	8,70	33,69	c	Tp Ns	1 VI	66° 42'	10° 30' E.	8,58	34,69	cc	T Tp Ns
28 V	58° 14'	4° 40' E.	8,8	31,83	+	Ns Tp	2 VI	68° 30'	13° 10' E.	7,55	34,33	+	Ns C
29 V	60° 13'	4° 24' E.	8,95	33,32	r	Ns Tp	2 VI	68° 49'	13° 50' E.	7,70	34,16	r	C Ns
30 V	62° 41'	5° E.	7,47	33,12	+	Ns Tp	2 IX	75° 50'	15° 32' E.	5,52	35,01		S T
30 V	63° 13'	5° 15' E.	8,14	34,53	+	Tp Ns	4 IX	73° 36'	18° 50' E.	7,06	35,03	+	S (Ns)
30 V	63° 52'	6° 5' E.	8,00	34,53	+	Tp Ns	4 IX	72° 43'	16° 43' E.	8,80	35,01	r	Tp Ns
31 V	65° 19'	6° 20' E.	8,35	35,34	+	—	6 IX	70° 23'	20° 32' E.	9,37	34,41	+	Tp Ns
31 V	65° 47'	9° 10' E.	9,01	34,57	+	Ns Tp							

P. divergens EHB.

Surface:

Date.	Lat. N.	Long.	Temp.	Sal.	Fq.	Pl.
29 VIII	77° 38'	11° 40' E.	6	34,89	r	S T
4 IX	73° 43'	16° 43' E.	8,6	35,01	c	Tp Ns
5 IX	71° 14'	16° 38' E.	9,40	34,92	+	Tp Ns

P. ovatum POUCHET.

Surface:

Date.	Lat. N.	Long.	Temp.	Sal.	Fq.	Pl.
29 V	61° 40'	4° 20' E.	7,05	33,47	r	Ns Tp
30 V	68° 52'	6° 5' E.	8	34.53	r	Tp Ns
31 V	65° 34'	8° 45' E.	8,83	35,00	r	Ns T
31 V	65° 47'	9° 10' E.	9,01	34,67	r	Ns (Tp)
1 VI	66° 42'	10° 30' E.	8,53	34,69	+	T Tp Ns
2 VI	68° 30'	13° 10' E.	7,55	34,33	r	Ns C
21 VI	76° 27'	25° 55' E.	0,24	33,68	r	(C)
21 VIII	80° 31'	18° 50' E.	2,42	33,93	r	Ng
29 VIII	77° 38'	11° 40' E.	6	34,89	r	T S
31 VIII	76° 27'	10° 43' E.	5,35	35,03	r	S
1 IX	76° 2'	13° 8' E.	6,61	35,13	r	S T
2 IX	75° 50'	15° 32' E.	5,52	35,01	r	S T
4 IX	72° 43'	18° 43' E.	8,8	35,01	r	Tp Ns

P. pellucidum BERGH.

Surface:

Date.	Lat. N.	Long.	Temp.	Sal.	Fq.	Pl.	Date.	Lat. N.	Long.	Temp.	Sal.	Fq.	Pl.
21 VI	76° 27'	25° 55' E.	0,24	33,68	+	(C)	18 VIII	79° 55'	32° 10' E.	—0,58	33,21	+	Ng C
25 VI	76° 34'	17° 24' E.	0,6	33,30	+	—	19 VIII	80° 27'	30° 15' E.	—0,90	32,03	+	Ng
26 VI	76° 46'	15° 22' E	0,95	34,04	r	—	20 VIII	81° 14'	22° 50' E.	1,18	33,42	r	T
26 VII	78° 13'	7° 30' E.	5,34	34,89	r	—	20 VIII	80° 45'	26° 40' E.	0,13	32,20	+	(Ng)
26 VII	77° 53'	5° 3' E	4.78	34,57	r	((C))	20 VIII	81° 8'	23° 35' E.	0,71	32,84	c	(Ng)
30 VII	75° 12'	0° 17' W.	4,59	34,53	c	(C)	21 VIII	80° 31'	18° 50' E.	2,42	33,93	c	Ng T
3 VIII	77° 3'	23° 35' E.	3,94	34,45	r	(C)	25 VIII	79° 53'	11° 22' E.	2,77	33,75	+	C (S) Ng
3 VIII	77° 46'	26° 18' E.	1,28	30,98	+	C (Ng)	29 VIII	77° 23'	10° 53' E.	5,55	35,03	c	T S
4 VIII	78° 18'	28° E.	2,12	33,01	c	Ng C	31 VIII	76° 27'	10° 43' E.	5,35	35,03	c	S
16 VIII	78° 27'	32° 30' E.	1,52	33,46	+	Ng C	1 IX	76° 2'	13° 8' E.	6,61	35,13	c	S T

Phalacroma operculoides SCHÜTT.

Surface:

Date.	Lat. N.	Long.	Temp.	Sal.	Fq.	Pl.
29 VIII	77° 38'	11° 40' E.	6	34,89	r	T S
29 VIII	77° 23'	10° 53' E.	5,55	35,03	r	T S
31 VIII	76° 27'	10° 43' E.	5,35	35,03	r	S

Diatomaceæ.

Asteromphalus atlanticus CL.

Deep-sea haul: 29—30 VII. Lat. N. 78° 13'. Loung. W. 2° 58'. Depth. 500—0 m. Fq. rr.

Chætoceros atlanticus Cl.

Surface:

Date.	Lat. N.	Long.	Temp.	Sal.	Fq.	Pl.
2 VI	68° 30'	13° 10' E.	7,55	34,93	r	Ns S
12 VI	73° 40'	22° 40' E.	2,40	35,05	r	C
15 VIII	78° 38'	34° 30' E.	1,52	33,21	r	C
27 VIII	79° 58'	9° 35' E.	4,58	34,53	rr	T
29 VIII	77° 36'	11° 40' E.	6	31,89	r	S T
29 VIII	77° 23'	10° 53' E.	5,55	35,03	rr	S T
30 VIII	76° 45'	6° 45' E.	5,34	34,92	rr	S
1 IX	76° 2'	13° 8' E.	6,61	35,18	r	S T
3 IX	74° 42'	16° 42' E.	7,24	35,17	r	T(S)

C. borealis Btw.

Surface:

Date.	Lat. N.	Long.	Temp.	Sal.	Fq.	Pl.
30 V	63° 13'	5° 15' E.	8,17	34,53	r	Tp Ns
10 VI	71° 10'	21° 31' R.	6,71	35,20	+	C S
12 VI	73° 40'	22° 40' E.	2,40	35,05	r	C
23 VI	77° 15'	27° 10' E.	0,97	33,15	r	(C)
3 VIII	77° 46'	26° 18' E	1,23	30,98	r	(C)
15 VIII	77° 48'	32° 53' E.	1,55	33,20	r	(C)
15 VIII	78° 36'	34° 30' E.	1,52	33,21	c	C
20 VIII	81° 14'	22° 50' E.	1,18	33,42	c	T
20 VIII	81° 8'	23° 35' E.	0,71	32,84	+	Ng
21 VIII	80° 31'	18° 50' E.	2,42	33,93	+	Ng
25 VIII	79° 58'	11° 22' E.	2 77	33,75	r	C(S) Ng
27 VIII	79° 58'	9° 35' E.	4,58	34,53	r	T
1 IX	76° 2'	13° 8' E.	6,61	35,18	r	S T
2 IX	75° 24'	16° 47' E.	5,64	35,12	r	T(S)
4 IX	73° 36'	18° 50' E.	7,06	35,03	+	S (Ns)

C. borealis var. Brightwellii Cl.

Surface:

Date.	Lat. N.	Long.	Temp.	Sal.	Fq.	Pl.	Date.	Lat. N.	Long.	Temp.	Sal.	Fq.	Pl.
2 VI	68° 30'	13° 10' E.	7,55	34,93	rr	Ns C	1 IX	76° 2'	13° 8' E.	6,61	35,18	+	S T
10 VI	71° 42'	22° 35' E.	6,40	35,15	+	T C S	2 IX	75° 24'	16° 47' E.	5,64	35,12	r	T(S)
20 VIII	81° 14'	22° 50' E.	1,18	33,42	c	T	3 IX	74° 42'	16° 42' E.	7,24	35,17	c	T(S)
24 VIII	80° 8'	16° 32' E.	3,44	33,59	r	Ng	4 IX	73° 36'	18° 50' E.	7,06	35,03	r	S (Ns)
27 VIII	79° 58'	9° 35' E.	4,58	34,53	+	T	4 IX	72° 43'	18° 43' E.	8,8	35,01	r	Tp Ns
31 VIII	76° 12'	12° 18' E.	6,20	35,15	r	S							

C. borealis var. solitaria CL.

Surface:

Date.	Lat. N.	Long.	Temp.	Sal.	Fq.	Pl.
9 VI	70° 54'	20° 43' E.	7,15	34,83	+	C S
10 VI	71° 42'	22° 35' E.	6,40	35,15	+	T C N
29 VIII	77° 23'	10° 53' B.	5,55	35,03	+	S T
30 VIII	76° 45'	8° 43' E.	5,34	34,92	c	S
31 VIII	76° 27'	10° 43' E.	5,35	35,03	+	S
2 IX	75° 24'	16° 47' E.	5,64	35,12	r	T (S)

C. contortus SCHÜTT.

Deep-sea haul: 27 VIII. Lat. N. 79° 58'. Long E. 9° 35'. Depth 400—0 m. Fq. r.
        5 IX. » » 71° 50'. » » 18° 2'. » 20—0 » » r.

C. eriophilus CASTR.

Surface:

Date.	Lat. N.	Long.	Temp.	Sal.	Fq.	Pl.	Date.	Lat. N.	Long.	Temp.	Sal.	Fq.	Pl.
2 VI	68° 30'	13° 10' E.	7,55	34,33	r	Ns C	27 VIII	70° 58'	9° 35' E.	4,58	34,68	c	T
2 VI	68° 49'	13° 50' E.	7,70	34,16	c	C Ns	29 VIII	77° 38'	11° 40' E.	6	34,89	+	S T
9 VI	70° 54'	20° 43' E.	7,15	34,83	+	C S	29 VIII	77° 23'	10° 53' E.	5,55	35,03	c	S T
10 VI	71° 10'	21° 31' E.	6,71	35,20	r	C S	31 VIII	76° 12'	12° 18' E.	6,26	35,15	+	S
10 VI	71° 42'	22° 35' E.	6,40	35,15	c	T C S	1 IX	76° 2'	13° 8' E.	6,61	35,13	c	S T
20 VIII	81° 14'	22° 50' E.	1,16	33,42	c	T	2 IX	75° 24'	16° 47' E.	5,64	35,12	c	T (S)
20 VIII	81° 8'	23° 35' E.	0,71	32,64	»	Ng	3 IX	74° 42'	16° 42' E.	7,24	35,17	+	T (S)
24 VIII	80° 6'	16° 32' E.	3,14	33,59	r	Ng	4 IX	73° 36'	18° 50' E.	7,06	35,03	r	S (Ns)
25 VIII	79° 53'	11° 22' E.	2,77	33,75	r	C (S) Ng							

C. debilis CL.

Haul: 27 VIII. Lat. N. 79° 58'. Long E. 9° 35'. Depth 400—0 m. Fq. r.

C. decipiens CL.

Surface:

Date.	Lat. N.	Long.	Temp.	Sal.	Fp.	Pl.	Date.	Lat. N.	Long.	Temp.	Sal.	Fq.	Pl.
2 VI	68° 30'	13° 10' E.	7,55	34,33	+	Ns C	30 VII	78° 12'	0° 17' W.	4,59	34,52	+	(C)
2 VI	68° 49'	13° 50' E.	7,70	34,16	c	C Ns	3 VIII	77° 3'	28° 35' E.	3,94	34,45	r	(C)
9 VI	70° 54'	20° 43' E.	7,15	34,83	c	C S	3 VIII	77° 46'	26° 18' E.	1,23	30,98	c	C Ng
10 VI	71° 10'	21° 31' E.	6,71	35,20	+	C S	4 VIII	78° 18'	26° E.	2,12	33,01	r	Ng C
10 VI	71° 42'	22° 35' E.	6,40	35,15	c	C T S	15 VIII	77° 48'	32° 53' E.	1,55	33,20	+	(C)
11 VI	73° 10'	21° 46' E.	5,58	35,26	+	(C ?)	15 VIII	78° 38'	34° 30' E.	1,52	33,21	cc	C
11 VI	73° 3'	23° 28' E.	5,15	35,37	c	C	16 VIII	78° 27'	32° 30' E.	1,52	33,46	r	Ng C
12 VI	73° 40'	22° 40' E.	3,40	35,05	cc	C	18 VIII	79° 55'	32° 10' E.	—0,58	33,21	r	Ng C
23 VI	77° 15'	27° 10' E.	0,97	33,15	+	(C)	25 VIII	79° 53'	11° 22' E.	2,77	33,75	+	C (S) Ng
26 VII	77° 53'	5° 3' E.	4,76	34,57	+	(C)	27 VIII	79° 58'	9° 35' E.	4,58	34,53	r	T
28 VII	77° 52'	3° 5' W.	3,63	34,88	+	C	4 IX	72° 43'	18° 43' E.	8,8	35,01	r	Ty Ns

C. diadema (EHB.).

Surface:

Date.	Lat. N.	Long.	Temp.	Sal.	Fq.	Pl.
28 VII	77° 52′	3° 5′ W.	8,63	34,38	r	C Ng
20 VIII	81° 14′	22° 50′ E.	1,16	33,42	r	T
25 VIII	79° 58′	11° 22′ E.	2,77	33,75	+	C (S) Ng
27 VIII	79° 58′	9° 35′ E.	4,58	34,53	c	T
29 VIII	77° 38′	11° 40′ E.	6	34,89	+	T S
1 IX	76° 2′	13° 8′ E.	6,61	35,13	r	T S

C. furcellatus BAIL.

Surface:

Date.	Lat. N.	Long.	Temp.	Sal.	Fq.	Pl.
12 VI	73° 40′	22° 40′ E.	2,40	35,05	+	C (Ng)
26 VI	76° 46′	15° 22′ E.	0,95	34,04	,	—
28 VII	77° 52′	3° 5′ W.	3,63	34,38	r	C Ng
25 VIII	79° 58′	11° 22′ E.	2,77	33,75	+	C (S) Ng

C. hiemalis CL. — The *C. didymus* var. *hiemalis* CL. (Phytoplakton of the Atlantic 21, Pl. I, fig. 18) cannot be considered as a more variety of *C. didymus*. Perhaps identical with *C. brevis* SCHÜTT.

Surface: 1 IX. Lat. N. 76° 2′. Long. E. 13° 8′. Temp. 6,61. Sal. 35,13. Fq. *r*. Pl. *S T*.

C. laciniosus SCHÜTT.

Deep-sea haul: 1 IX. Lat. N. 75° 50′. Long. E. 15° 25′. Depth. 325—0 m. Fq. *r*.

C. teres CL.

Surface:

Date.	Lat. N.	Long.	Temp.	Sal.	Fq.	Pl.
12 VI	73° 40′	22° 40′ E.	2,40	35,05	r	C
25 VIII	79° 58′	11° 22′ E.	2,77	33,75	+	C (S) Ng
27 VIII	79° 58′	9° 35′ E.	4,58	34,58	r	T
29 VIII	77° 38′	11° 40′ E.	6	34,89	r	S T

C. volans SCHÜTT. — Having had an opportunity of examining original specimens of *C. volans* I have been convinced of its identity with *C. currens* CL., which latter name must be abolishd.

Surface:

Date.	Lat. N.	Long.	Temp.	Sal.	Fq.	Pl.
9 VI	70° 54'	20°43' E.	7,15	34,83	c	C S
31 VII	77° 14'	6°34' E.	5,35	34,77	c	S
1 VIII	76° 36'	12° 8' E.	7,38	35,12	+	S T
29 VIII	77° 38'	11°40' E.	6	34,89	r	T S
29 VIII	77° 23'	10°53' E.	5,55	35,03	c	T S
30 VIII	77	8° 3' E.	5,65	35,03	c	S
30 VIII	76° 45'	8°45' E.	5,34	34,92	c	S
31 VIII	76° 27'	10°43' E.	5,35	35,03	cc	S
2 IX	75° 24'	16°47' E.	5,64	35,12	+	T (S)

Corethron hystrix HENSEN. — This species is probably identical with *C. criophilum* CASTR. from the Antarctic Ocean. According to a recent publication of Dr. LEUDUGER FORTMOREL * this species occurs West of Africa in the region of Cape Verde together with *Chætoceros scolopendra* CL. (= *C. spinosum* LEUD.). Both are found also by me in a gathering (March 1898) from the same region. In March and April 1898 this species was found, besides, in the region of the Canaries and from the Azores to the mouth of the English Channel, in June and July around the Shetlands. In case C. hystrix be identical with C. criophilum this form goes thus, following the western coast of Africa, from the Antarctic to the Arctic region. It has also (once in March 1898) been seen North of the South American coast, but not in the intermediate region of the Sargasso Sea. The *Corethron hystrix*, although in general of rare occurrence, is a species of considerable interest and belongs evidently to the styliplankton.

Surface:

Date.	Lat. N.	Long.	Temp.	Sal.	Fq.	Pl.
29 VIII	77° 38'	11°40' E.	6	34,89	rr	T S
29 VIII	77° 23'	10°53' E.	5,55	35,03	r	T S
31 VIII	76° 26'	10°43' E.	5,35	35,03	r	S
1 IX	76° 2'	13° 6' E.	6,61	35,13	c	S T
2 IX	75° 24'	16°47' E.	5,64	35,12	r	T (S)
6 IX	70° 23'	20°32' E.	9,37	34,41	r	Tp Ns

Coscinodiscus oculus iridis EHB.

Surface:

Date.	Lat. N.	Long.	Temp.	Sal.	Fq.	Pl.	Date.	Lat. N.	Long.	Temp.	Sal.	Fq.	Pl.
30 V	63° 13'	5°15' E.	8,17	34,53	r	Tp Ns	29 VI	77° 15'	27°10' E.	0,97	33,15	c	C T
10 VI	71 10'	21°31' E.	6,71	35,20	+	C S	3 VIII	77 16'	26°18' E.	1,23	30,98	+	C (Ng)
12 VI	73° 40'	22°40' E.	2,40	35,05	r	C	15 VIII	78° 38'	34°30' E.	1,52	32,21	r	C
23 VI	77° 25'	27 30' E.	—0,35	32,97	+	—	16 VIII	78° 27'	32 30' E.	1,52	33,46	r	C Ng
23 VI	77 15'	27°10' E.	0,97	33,15	+	—	2 IX	75° 50'	15°32' E.	5,52	35,01	r	T S

* Diatomées marines de la côte occidentale d'Afrique. S:t Brieux 1898. 4:o.

Leptocylindrus danicus CL.

Surface:

Date.	Lat. N.	Long.	Temp.	Sal.	Fq.	Pl.
30 V	63° 13'	5° 15' E.	8,17	34,53	c	Tp Ns
20 VIII	81° 14'	22° 50' E.	1,18	33,42	r	T
20 VIII	81° 8'	23° 35' E.	0,71	32,84	r	Ng
21 VIII	80° 31'	18° 50' E.	2,42	33,93	r	Ng T
27 VIII	79° 58'	9° 35' E.	4,58	34,53	r	T

Rhizosolenia alata BTW.

Surface:

Date.	Lat. N.	Long.	Temp.	Sal.	Fq.	Pl.
30 VIII	76° 45'	8° 45' E.	5,34	34,92	+	S
4 IX	72° 43'	18° 43' E.	8,8	35,01	r	Tp Ns
5 IX	71° 57'	19° E.	9,08	34,96	r	Tp (Ns)

R(alata var.) gracillima CL.

Surface:

Date.	Lat. N.	Long.	Temp.	Sal.	Fq.	Pl.
31 VII	77° 14'	6° 34' E.	5,35	34,77	c	S
25 VIII	79° 58'	11° 22' E.	2,77	33,75	r	C (S) Ng
27 VIII	79° 58'	9° 35' E	4,58	34,53	+	T
30 VIII	76° 45'	8° 45' E.	5,34	34,92	c	S
31 VIII	76° 27'	10° 43' R.	5,35	35,03	r	S
31 VIII	76° 12'	12° 18' E.	6,26	35,15	+	S
4 IX	72° 43'	18° 43' E.	8,8	35,01	r	Tp Ns
5 IX	71° 57'	19° E.	9,08	34,96	c	Tp (Ns)

R. hebetata BAIL.

Surface:

Date.	Lat. N.	Long.	Temp.	Sal.	Fq.	Pl.
27 VIII	79° 58'	9° 35' E.	4,58	34,53	r	T (S)
29 VIII	77° 38'	11° 40' E.	6	34,89	+	T S
29 VIII	77° 23'	10° 53' E.	5,56	35,03	r	T S
30 VIII	77°	8° 3' E.	5,65	35,03	c	S
30 VIII	76° 45'	8° 45' E.	5,34	34,92	c	S
31 VIII	76° 27'	10° 43' E.	5,35	35,08	r	S
31 VIII	76° 12'	12° 18' E.	6,26	35,15	r	S
1 IX	76° 2'	13° 8' E.	6,61	35,13	+	S T
2 IX	75° 24'	16° 47' E.	5,64	35,12	+	T (S)
3 IX	74° 42'	16° 42' E.	7,24	35,17	+	T (S)
5 IX	71° 57'	19° E.	9,08	34,96	r	Tp (Ns)

R. obtusa Hensen.

Surface:

Date.	Lat. N.	Long.	Temp.	Sal.	Fq.	Pl.
12 VI	73° 40'	22° 40' E.	2,40	35,05	r	C
20 VIII	81° 14'	22° 50' E.	1,18	33,42	+	T
20 VIII	81° 8'	23° 35' E.	0,71	32,84	+	Ng
21 VIII	80° 31'	18° 50' E.	2,42	33,93	+	Ng T
29 VIII	77° 38'	11° 40' E	6	34,89	r	T S
29 VIII	77° 23'	10° 53' E.	5,55	35,03	c	T S
31 VIII	76° 12'	12° 18' E.	6,26	35,15	r	S
1 IX	76° 2'	13° 8' E.	6,61	35,13	r	S T

R. semispina Hensen.

Surface:

Date.	Lat. N.	Long.	Temp.	Sal.	Fq.	Pl.
30 V	63° 13'	5° 15' E.	8,17	34,53	rr	Tp Ns
9 VI	70° 54'	20° 43' E.	7,15	34,83	+	C S
10 VI	71° 10'	21° 31' E.	6,71	35,20	+	C S
10 VI	71° 42'	22° 35' E.	6,40	35,15	cc	T C S
20 VIII	81° 14'	22° 50' E.	1,18	33,42	r	T
30 VIII	77°	8° 3' E.	5,65	35,03	r	S

R. styliformis Btw.

Surface:

Date.	Lat. N.	Long.	Temp.	Sal.	Fq.	Pl.
27 V	57° 50'	6° E.	8,70	33,69	r	Tp Ns
30 V	63° 13'	5° 15' E.	8,17	34,53	rr	Tp Ns
27 VIII	79° 58'	9° 35' E.	4.58	34,53	r	T (C)
29 VIII	77° 38'	11° 40' E.	6	34,89	r	S T
30 VIII	76° 45'	8° 45' E.	5,34	34,89	+	S
2 IX	75° 50'	15° 32' E.	3,52	35,01	r	S T
2 IX	75° 24'	16° 47' E.	5,64	35,12	r	T (S)
3 IX	74° 42'	16° 42' E.	7,21	35,17	r	T (S)
4 IX	73° 36'	18° 50' E.	7,06	35,03	c	S (Ns)

Thalassiosira gravida Cl.

Surface:

Date.	Lat. N.	Long.	Temp.	Sal.	Fq.	Pl.	Date.	Lat. N.	Long.	Temp.	Sal.	Fq.	Pl.
12 VI	73° 40'	22° 40' E.	2,40	35,05	r	C (Ng)	25 VIII	79° 53'	11° 22' E.	3,77	33,75	+	C (S) Ng
20 VIII	81° 14'	22° 50' E.	1,18	33,42	+	T	27 VIII	79° 58'	9° 35' E.	4,58	34,53	c	T (S)
20 VIII	81° 8'	23° 35' E.	0,71	32,84	+	Ng	29 VIII	77° 38'	11° 40' E	6	34,89	r	T S
21 VIII	80° 31'	18° 50' E.	2,42	33,93	+	Ng T							

T. Nordenskiöldii CL.

Surface:

Date.	Lat. N.	Long.	Temp.	Sal.	Fq.	Pl.
25 VI	76° 34'	17° 24' E.	0,6	33,80	+	((C))
28 VII	77° 52'	3° 5' E.	3,03	34,38	r	C(Ng)

Thalassiothrix longissima CL. & GRUN.

Surface:

Date.	Lat. N.	Long.	Temp.	Sal.	Fq.	Pl.
10 VI	71° 10'	21° 31' E.	6,71	35,20	r	C S
31 VIII	76° 12'	12° 18' E.	6,26	35,15	?	S
1 IX	76° 2'	13° 8' E.	6,61	35,18	r	S T
3 IX	74° 42'	16° 42' E.	7,24	35,17	+	T(S)

The scarcity in 1898 of this and the precedent species, in other years usually very abundant in the Arctic Ocean and the Northern Atlantic, is really striking.

Plate I.

			Pag.
Fig.	1.	Fungella arctica CL.	22.
»	2.	Tintinnus (?) calyptra CL.	24.
»	3.	Tintinnus minutus BRANDT.	24.
»	4.	Tintinnus (?) pellucidus CL.	24.
»	5.	Actinomma boreale CL. *a* Primordial shell, *b* Secundary (Haliomma-)shell, *c* Tertiary (Actinomma-) shell, *d* Structure of *c*	26.
»	6.	Artrostrobus annulatus BAIL.	27.
»	7.	Aulacantha lævissima HKL.	27.
»	8.	Deroetta melo CL.	27.
»	9.	Challengeron Nathorstii CL. *a* Entire shell, *b* Structure	28.
»	10.	Botryopyle setosa CL. *a* Shell, *b* Septum	27.

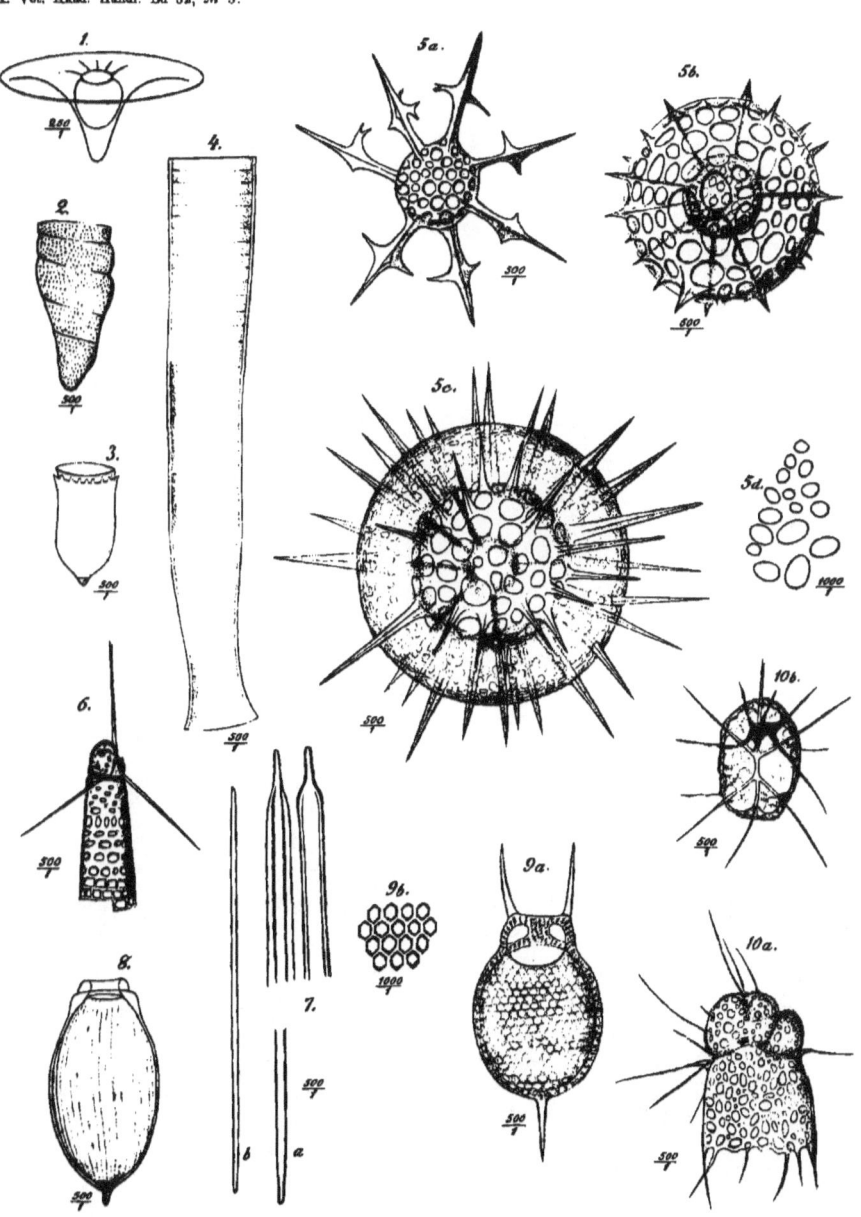

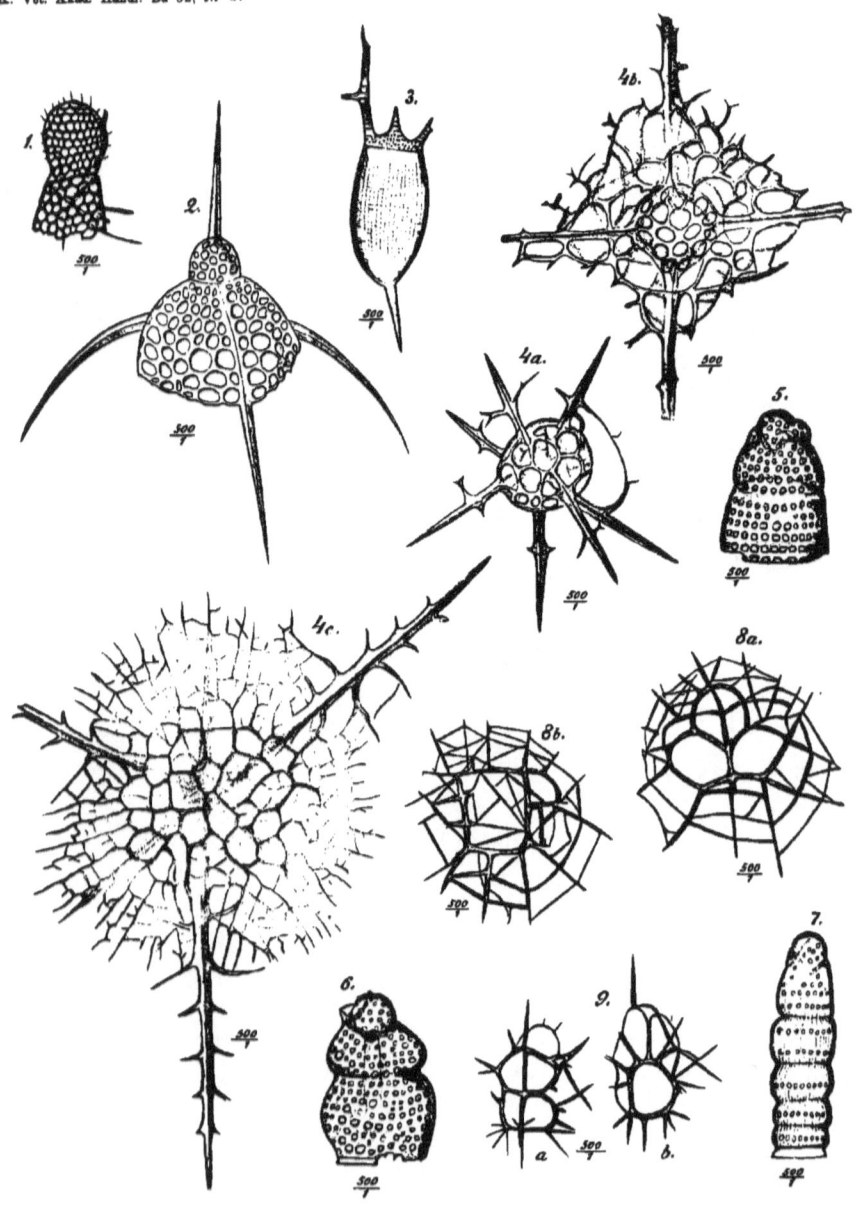

Plate II.

		Pag.
Fig. 1.	Dictyocephalus sp.?	29.
» 2.	Dictyophimus gracilipes BAIL..	29.
» 3.	Euphysetta Nathorstii CL.	29.
» 4.	Hexadoras borealis CL. *a* Primordial shell, *b* and *c* Outer shell in different state of development	30.
» 5.	Lithomitra australis EHB.?	30.
» 6.	Form allied to the precedent	30.
» 7.	Lithomitra lineata EHB.	30.
» 8.	Peridium (?) intricatum CL. *a* and *b* The shell in different foci	31.
» 9.	Peridium (?) laxum CL. *a* and *b* The shell in different foci	31.

Plate III.

		Pag.
Fig. 1.	Peridium (?) minutum CL. *b* and *c* The same shell in different foci	31.
» 2.	Phorticium pylonium HKL. *a, b, c* The shell in different state of development, *d* The primordial shell.	31.
» 3.	Plectanium (?) simplex CL.	32.
» 4.	Polypetta holostoma CL. *a* The shell, *b* Structure	32.
» 5.	Theocorys borealis CL.	33.

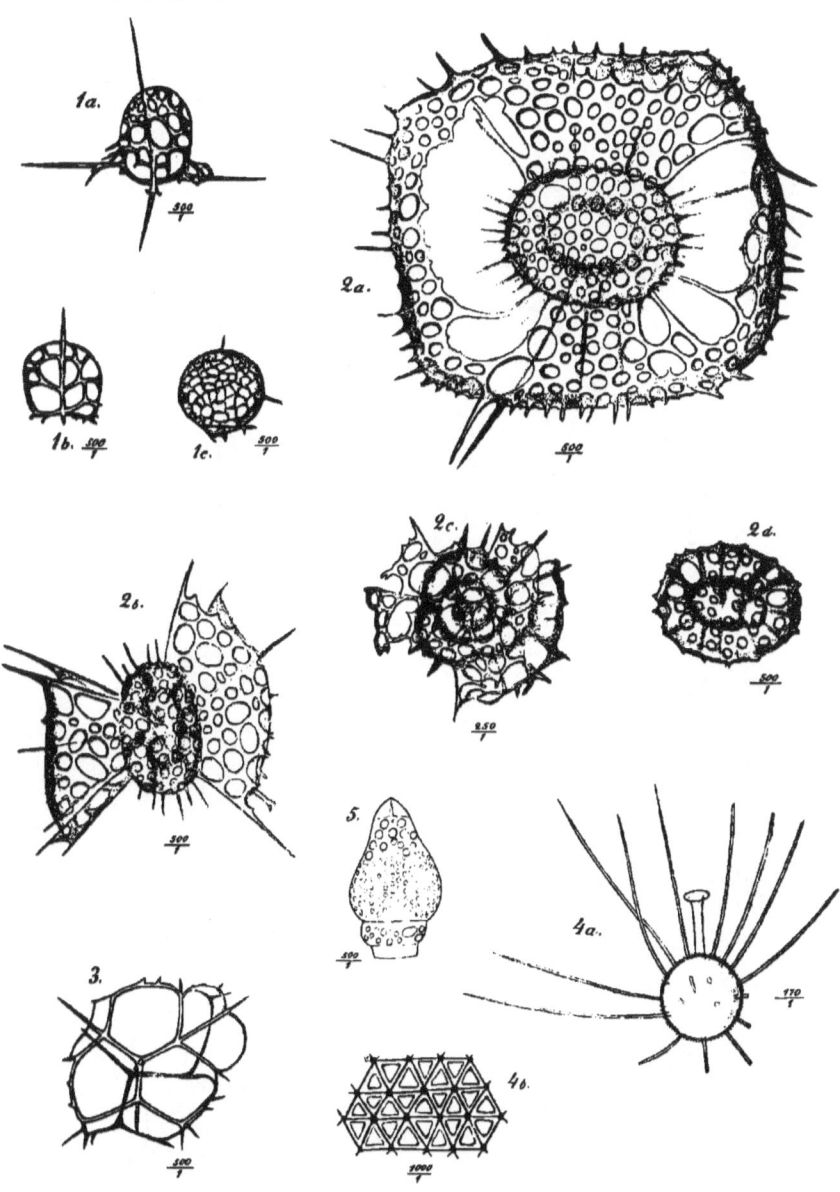

Pl. III.

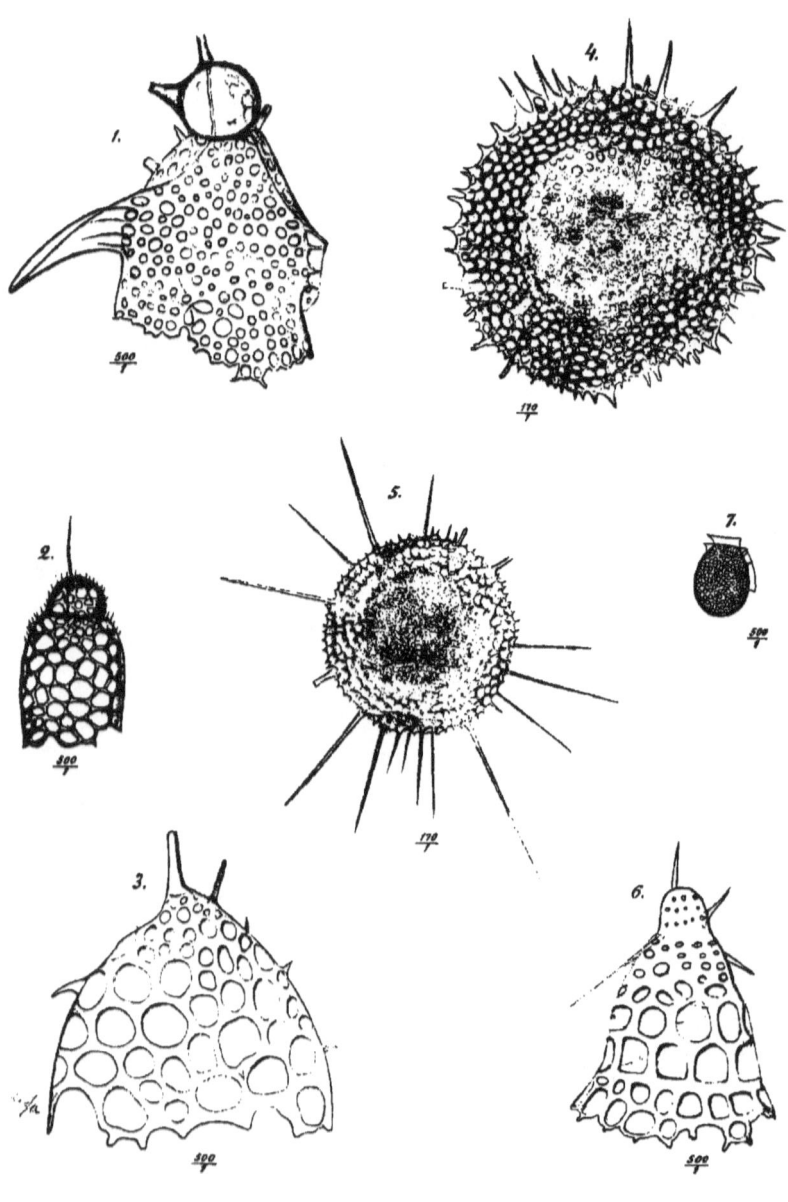

Plate IV.

Fig. 1. Pterocorys irregularis CL.
» 2. Sethoconus tabulatus (EHB.)
» 3. Sethoconus galea CL.
» 4. Trochodiscus echinidiscus HKL.
5. Trochodiscus helioides CL.
» 6. Stichopilium davisianum (EHB.)
» 7. Dinophysis granulata CL.

www.ingramcontent.com/pod-product-compliance
Lightning Source LLC
Chambersburg PA
CBHW020157170426
43199CB00010B/1076